Balance Screen Time With Green Time

For my parents, Jim and Vonda Stevens,
for filling my childhood with nature.

Balance Screen Time With Green Time

Connecting Students With Nature

Emily Morgan

CORWIN
A SAGE Publishing Company

A SAGE Publishing Company

For information:

Corwin
A SAGE Company
2455 Teller Road
Thousand Oaks, California 91320
(800) 233-9936
www.corwin.com

SAGE Publications Ltd.
1 Oliver's Yard
55 City Road
London, EC1Y 1SP
United Kingdom

SAGE Publications India Pvt. Ltd.
Unit No 323-333, Third Floor,
F-Block
International Trade Tower
Nehru Place
New Delhi – 110 019
India

SAGE Publications Asia-
Pacific Pte. Ltd.
18 Cross Street #10-10/11/12
China Square Central
Singapore 048423

Vice President and Editorial Director:
    Monica Eckman
Publisher: Jessica Allan
Content Development Editor:
    Mia Rodriguez
Senior Editorial Assistant:
    Natalie Delpino
Editorial Intern: Lex Nunez
Production Editor: Tori Mirsadjadi
Copy Editor: Colleen Brennan
Typesetter: Integra
Cover Designer: Scott Van Atta
Marketing Manager: Olivia Bartlett

Printed in the United States of America.

Paperback ISBN 9781071912201

This book is printed on acid-free paper.

23 24 25 26 27 10 9 8 7 6 5 4 3 2 1

CONTENTS

Visit the companion website at
resources.corwin.com/BalanceScreenTimeWithGreenTime
for downloadable resources.

NOTE FROM THE PUBLISHER: The author has provided links to video and web content throughout the book that are available to you through QR (quick response) codes. To read a QR code, you must have a smartphone or tablet with a camera. We recommend that you download a QR code reader app that is made specifically for your phone or tablet brand.

Links may also be accessed at **resources.corwin.com/BalanceScreen TimeWithGreenTime**

PREFACE

Ever since I was a little girl, I have loved being outside and learning about nature. My dad, a high school science teacher, and my mom, lover of plants and animals, taught us to garden, took us on countless camping trips, and encouraged us to learn and play outdoors. I remember with fondness a Weeping Willow tree in the backyard that, when we parted its curtain of branches, transported my sisters and me to our own special place that seemed miles away from "the real world." I count my childhood time in nature as one of the most precious gifts my parents have given me. The feelings of awe and comfort I experienced in nature when I was young I still experience today. And as my adult world has become louder, more hectic, and more complicated, time in nature has become even more important to me.

For the past 17 years, I have been traveling the country sharing lessons focused on teaching STEM (science, technology, engineering, and math). Honestly, I get as excited about technology and engineering as I do about nature. I am married to an engineer and the mom of a teenager who is crazy about robotics, so technology is often the topic of conversation at home. We marvel at the technological advances that seem to happen almost daily and appreciate how they have made our lives better. As an educator, I am astounded by the incredible learning opportunities the newest technologies provide, and I appreciate how technology allowed us to stay connected with our students during a pandemic.

But in my work with schools and as a mother, I am noticing a quickly growing imbalance between the time students spend on screens and the time they spend outdoors. So I developed a teacher workshop called "Balance Screen Time With Green Time" to help teachers find ways to easily incorporate nature time into a traditional school day. I was encouraged by the positive response from the workshops and wanted to share these strategies with a wider audience of educators. That's why I wrote this book—to share with you the many benefits of getting students outdoors and simple strategies for doing so, all in an effort to balance screen time with some green time.

In Chapter 1, I'll share with you the many research-based benefits of green time. Chapter 2 introduces the idea of green breaks, which can be used to help your students (and you) renew, reset, and refresh throughout the school day. Chapter 3 offers 25 green break ideas you can use with students of any age as well as connections to curriculum to get you thinking about how you might extend that experience with nature. In Chapter 4 you'll read about educators who are finding creative and meaningful ways to get kids connected with nature. Chapter 5 is all about you—providing ideas for how you can incorporate more green time into your professional and personal life. And finally, there is an appendix of resources (websites, books, apps, programs, and professional learning opportunities) you might find helpful in your effort to incorporate green time.

My hope is that by making green time a regular part of our school days, students will develop a connection to nature that will last throughout their lives. Whether you decide to try some 10-minute "green breaks" or want to engage your students in a months-long "green project," every effort matters.

ACKNOWLEDGMENTS

I would like to express heartfelt thanks to the following people whose kind deeds, willingness to share, and supportive actions have made this book possible.

To Jessica Allan and Corwin for giving me the opportunity to share these ideas with educators and to Page Keeley for introducing us.

To Mia Rodriguez for your guidance through this process and for responding to my many emails with kindness and all the answers.

To Lucas Schleicher, Natalie Delpino, Tori Mirsadjadi, Colleen Brennan, Olivia Bartlett, and everyone I have interacted with at Corwin. You have all made this a wonderful experience.

To Scott Van Atta for designing a splendidly green book cover that exceeded my expectations.

To the educators who contributed their stories, ideas, and photographs. I have no doubt your contributions will inspire others. Most of all, thanks for the work you are doing day in and day out to connect kids with nature.

To Tom Uhlman for the photo shoot in the woods behind your home, for lying in the leaf litter to get just the right angle, and for making these photo sessions fun for everyone!

To my dear friend Terri Collins for supporting and sharing my work for all these years, for the many opportunities to work with preservice teachers (a.k.a. "your people"), and especially for the amazing wildlife adventures.

To Kim Stilwell for working hard to share my *Next Time You See* series and "Balance Screen Time With Green Time" teacher workshop. This book wouldn't have happened without your encouragement and support in those early days!

To Chris Lewis for inviting me to Kansas City to share an early version of my "Balance Screen Time With Green Time" workshop. Those two days outdoors with Blue Springs teachers were instrumental in developing and refining this concept.

To my mentor, Pat Terry, for your wisdom and encouragement all these years.

To Karen Ansberry, my Picture-Perfect Science partner, for all the years of encouragement on my solo projects and for the adventures we've had outdoors on our work trips.

To Chris Anderson and Liz Wolf for introducing me to amazing educators in Cincinnati Public Schools who are making green time happen for their students.

To Meredith Florkey at Ohio Naturally for sharing your expertise and for introducing me to the folks at Arlitt Child Development Center and the Nature Class teachers at Centerville City Schools.

To Rachel Konerman at Arlitt Child Development Center for showing me around your amazing school.

To Brenda Metcalf, executive director of the Environmental Education Council of Ohio, for introducing me to some outstanding environmental educators and for all you do to promote environmental education in our state.

To my parents, Jim and Vonda Stevens, for all the camping trips, gardening time, and boating adventures. Thanks for sending me outside to play all day until I heard Pop's whistle as the signal to come inside. Not until I was older did I realize how lucky I was to have all that time and freedom outdoors.

To my sister Julie for pointing out all the ordinary moments of "heaven" and my sister Angie for always encouraging me to follow my dreams.

To Jeff for your support and love at home and fun and laughs when we hit the trail. Thanks for making my backyard "sanctuary" vision a reality. Thank you for giving me the encouragement and time to write this book.

To Jack for the walks in the woods, the times I treasure most.

Publisher's Acknowledgments

Corwin gratefully acknowledges the contributions of the following reviewer:

Gaby Scelfo
High School English Teacher
Academy of the Sacred Heart
Lafayette, LA

 Emily Morgan is a former elementary and middle school science teacher. She is the author of the *Next Time You See* picture book series for children and co-author of the *Picture-Perfect STEM Lessons* series for teachers. Her book *Next Time You See a Sunset* was selected for Story Time from Space, where it was read by astronaut Mark Vande Hei on the International Space Station and shared with children all over the globe. She has served as a science consultant for the Hamilton County Educational Service Center in Cincinnati, Ohio, as the science leader for the High AIMS Consortium, as board president of iSPACE: The STEM Learning Place, and is currently a STEM consultant for the Ohio Afterschool Network. Emily holds a bachelor's degree in education from Wright State University and a master's in education from the University of Dayton.

SECTION I

GREEN TIME

BENEFITS OF GREEN TIME

I love this face. (The child's, not the toad's.) Although the toad *is* pretty cute, I am referring to the look of awe and wonder on the child's face. This is my son, Jack, on a walk at a local park where he discovered this little toad on the path. He excitedly pointed it out to me and couldn't believe it when I picked it up and placed it in his hands. I quickly captured his expression with my phone and, even though it's a little blurry, it remains one of my favorite photos of him. As an educator, I have seen this look again and again on the faces of children as they make discoveries in nature. From the excitement of lifting up a rock to find roly-poly pill bugs scurrying underneath, to the surprise of noticing the Moon in a daytime sky, to the wonder in observing a spider weaving an intricate web, nature never runs out of ways to inspire joy and awe in children. Many of us have observed first-hand the positive effects nature has had on the children in our lives, but the evidence goes beyond our own observations and intuitions as teachers, parents, aunts, uncles, and grandparents. There is a robust body of research suggesting that time in nature is essential for our mental and physical health and can even improve learning. In this chapter and throughout this book, I refer to time in nature as "green time." Some of the research-based benefits of green time are highlighted in the following section.

The Research

GREEN TIME CAN RENEW ATTENTION

Researchers studying the effect of natural settings on attention have found positive results time and time again. A study investigating how time spent in school green spaces affects children's cognitive performance found that "natural environments in schools can help students with better recovery of their attention resources, as well as in feeling more restored and less stressed and fatigued" (Amicone, 2018, p. 13). Another study that measured classroom engagement after students spent time in nature found that the rate of teachers needing to redirect students after coming inside was cut almost in half, allowing teachers to teach for longer, uninterrupted periods of time (Kuo et al., 2018). These results are not surprising, because nature inherently provides all of the components of a restor- ative environment proposed by attention restoration theory (ART) (Kaplan & Kaplan 1989), which is described in detail in Chapter 2. Additionally, research suggests that contact with nature can help children with ADHD cope with their symptoms (DiCarmine & Berto, 2020) and that "'doses of nature' might serve as a safe, inexpensive, widely accessible new tool in the tool kit for managing ADHD symp- toms" (Taylor & Kuo, 2009, p. 2).

GREEN TIME CAN IMPROVE LEARNING

The evidence that time in nature can support learning is strong, both in direct academic performance measures as well as essen- tial learning skills. A synthesis of research around nature-based learning shows a prevalence of positive impacts on academic outcomes with the highest level of positive results in the area of science, followed by math and language arts (Williams & Dixon, 2013). In another review of literature about nature-based learning programs, researchers found, "Report after report—from independent observers as well as participants themselves—indicate shifts in perseverance, problem solving, critical thinking, leadership, teamwork, and resilience" (Kuo et al., 2019, p. 1). These skills are essential to deep learning and cross all content areas. These findings have been consistently positive across diverse populations, instructors, instructional approaches, and educational settings (Kuo et al., 2019).

Source: iStock.com/RyanJLane

GREEN TIME CAN LOWER STRESS

Numerous studies show the stress-reducing effects of nature. The impact of natural settings on stress levels can be measured by using heart rates and stress hormone (cortisol) levels before and after time spent in nature. A 2019 study suggests taking at least 20 minutes out of your day to stroll or sit in a place that makes you feel in contact with nature can significantly lower your stress hormone levels. After 20 to 30 minutes sitting or walking in a natural area, cortisol levels dropped at their greatest rate. After that, additional de-stressing benefits continue to add up but at a slower rate (Hunter et al., 2019). Another study showed that participants who spent just 5 minutes sitting in nature experienced an increase in positive emotions (Neill et al., 2019).

Source: iStock.com/SolStock

GREEN TIME CAN LEAD TO MORE ENGAGEMENT

It makes sense that renewed attention, reduction in stress, and positive emotions would lead to more engagement from students, and research supports this notion. Teachers, and students themselves, report higher levels of engagement in learning when classes are taken outdoors as well as a higher degree of long-term knowledge retention (Fagerstam & Blom, 2013). These benefits seem especially present in students who are typically less motivated, and they appear throughout the grade levels (Detweiler et al., 2015). One study found that middle school students who previously viewed school-based learning as meaningless and disengaging were motivated and actively involved when participating in a field-based learning experience (James & Williams, 2017).

GREEN TIME FOSTERS IMPROVED BEHAVIOR

Natural settings have been shown to nurture better behavior. It is no surprise that if students are more engaged and less stressed, behavior will improve. A study involving elementary-aged students found that time spent in green and blue (beaches) spaces has been associated with fewer behavioral difficulties, a decrease in emotional symptoms, and a reduction in peer relationship trouble (Amoly et al., 2014). A study involving secondary students with behavior issues taking part in a 2-year gardening program showed that this regular exposure to nature over an extended period of time was associated with a decrease of disruptive behavior and lower dropout rates (Ruiz-Gallardo et al., 2013).

Source: iStock.com/kali9

GREEN TIME ADVANCES SOCIAL SKILLS

Studies have shown positive links between nature-based early childhood programs and improved social skills and better self-regulation (Johnstone et al., 2022). Green time promotes growth in social skills through providing opportunities that require prosocial peer-to-peer interactions and student-teacher interactions. Positive outcomes in social and emotional development for youth experiencing homelessness were found in an outdoor adventure–based program, with students specifically reporting that they felt more socially competent through experiences of giving and receiving social support (Parry et al., 2021). Extended time in nature, away from screens, has shown to improve preteens' skills with recognizing and understanding nonverbal emotional cues and therefore enhancing engagement with their peers in real-time, face-to-face interactions (Uhls et al., 2014).

GREEN TIME ENHANCES PHYSICAL HEALTH

Being outdoors can enhance our physical health by giving us opportunities to be more active than sitting at a desk indoors, and provides a free source of much needed vitamin D from the Sun. Spending time outdoors can even affect our sight. Research suggests that increasing the amount of time that children spend outdoors can reduce the risk of developing myopia (nearsightedness) (French et al., 2013; Xiong et al., 2017). And regular exposure to nature can lead to improved immune function (Frumpkin et al., 2017).

GREEN TIME CAN IMPROVE MENTAL HEALTH

Regular exposure to green spaces has been shown to reduce anxiety and boost mood in adolescents and young adults (Bray et al., 2022). Research from the Greater Good Science Center at UC Berkeley suggests that the awe often felt when immersed in nature can play a key role in recovery from trauma (Anderson et al., 2018). Likewise, studies show that experiences in nature can promote resilience and help with recovery from adverse childhood experiences (ACEs) (Poulson et al., 2020; Touloumakos & Barrable, 2020).

GREEN TIME FOSTERS CONNECTIONS WITH NATURE

Source: iStock.com/Caiaimage/Robert Daly

Time in nature can result in students feeling more connected to the natural world. One review of literature looked at arts-based nature activities in particular and found that in all eight studies reviewed, the top outcome reported was increased student connectivity to nature (Mouzla et al., 2022). Likewise, a study where participants spent time in "mundane nature" (also phrased as "nearby nature") each day for 5 days, focusing on the positive attributes of that natural space, showed increased connectedness to nature (Richardson et al., 2015).

GREEN TIME ENCOURAGES PRO-ENVIRONMENTAL BEHAVIORS

The two biggest factors that lead to pro-environmental attitudes and actions in adulthood are time in nature during childhood and the presence of role models who care for nature (Charles et al., 2018). Time playing in nature in early childhood contributes to attitudes of stewardship toward nature (Ernst et al., 2021). And personal connections with nature, along with meaning-focused coping skills (i.e., the belief that our actions can make a difference), can foster hope when children face fears and worries about the environment (Chawla, 2020).

Source: iStock.com/Motortion

I've briefly summarized some of the research around green time in the previous pages, but you should know that there is much more! An abundance of studies from all around the world support the benefits of green time, so many in fact that it can be overwhelming to sift through them all. The best resource I have found for navigating this field of research is the Children & Nature Network's (C&NN) Research Library, which is curated by the C&NN Scientific Advisory Council. You can easily search by topic to find the studies that apply to your unique learners and setting. The Resources section of the C&NN website provides webinars, case studies, videos, infographics, and other tools. The infographics can be especially useful when sharing the benefits of green time with others in your school, district, or community. These colorful one-page documents clearly and simply explain many of the research-based benefits of time spent in nature. Scan the QR code on this page to download the C&NN infographics.

bit.ly/3Q0EGLB

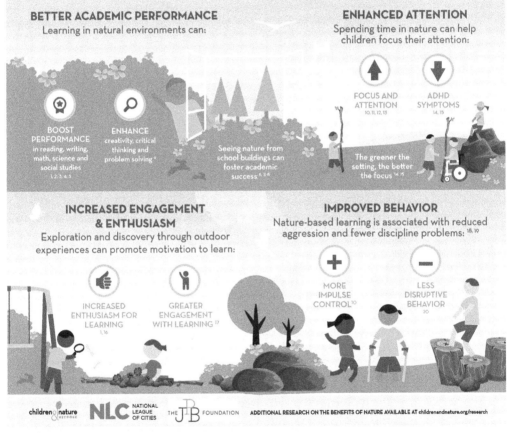

NATURE CAN IMPROVE ACADEMIC OUTCOMES

Spending time in nature enhances educational outcomes by improving children's academic performance, focus, behavior and love of learning.

BETTER ACADEMIC PERFORMANCE
Learning in natural environments can:

BOOST PERFORMANCE in reading, writing, math, science and social studies [1,2,3,4,5]

ENHANCE creativity, critical thinking and problem solving [4]

Seeing nature from school buildings can foster academic success [6,2,6]

ENHANCED ATTENTION
Spending time in nature can help children focus their attention:

FOCUS AND ATTENTION [10,11,12,13]

ADHD SYMPTOMS [14,15]

The greener the setting, the better the focus [14,15]

INCREASED ENGAGEMENT & ENTHUSIASM
Exploration and discovery through outdoor experiences can promote motivation to learn:

INCREASED ENTHUSIASM FOR LEARNING [1,16]

GREATER ENGAGEMENT WITH LEARNING [17]

IMPROVED BEHAVIOR
Nature-based learning is associated with reduced aggression and fewer discipline problems: [18,19]

MORE IMPULSE CONTROL [10]

LESS DISRUPTIVE BEHAVIOR [20]

children & nature NETWORK   NLC NATIONAL LEAGUE OF CITIES   THE JPB FOUNDATION   ADDITIONAL RESEARCH ON THE BENEFITS OF NATURE AVAILABLE AT childrenandnature.org/research

SUPPORTING RESEARCH
[1] Lieberman & Hoody (1998). Closing the achievement gap: Using the environment as an integrating context for learning. Results of a Nationwide Study. San Diego: SEER. [2] Chawla (2015). Benefits of nature contact for children. J Plan Lit, 30(4), 433–452. [3] Berezowitz et al. (2015). School gardens enhance academic performance and dietary outcomes in children. J School Health, 85(8), 508–518. [4] Williams & Dixon (2012). Impact of garden-based learning on academic outcomes in schools: Synthesis of research between 1990 and 2010. Rev Educ Res, 83(2), 211–235. [5] Wells et al. (2015). The effects of school gardens on children's science knowledge: A randomized controlled trial of low-income elementary schools. Int J Sci Edu, 37(17), 2858–2878. [6] Li & Sullivan (2016). Impact of views to school landscapes on recovery from stress and mental fatigue. Landscape Urban Plan, 148, 149–158. [7] Wu et al. (2014) Linking student performance in Massachusetts elementary schools with the "greenness" of school surroundings using remote sensing. PLoS ONE 9(10): e108548. [8] Matsuoka, R. H. 2010. Student performance and high school landscapes. Landscape and Urban Planning 97 (4), 273–282. [9] Moore & Wong (1997). Natural Learning: Rediscovering Nature's Way of Teaching. Berkeley, CA: MIG Communications. [10] Faber Taylor et al. (2002). Views of nature and self-discipline: Evidence from inner-city children. J Environ Psy, 22, 49–63. [11] Mårtensson et al. (2009). Outdoor environmental assessment of attention promoting settings for preschool children. Health Place, 15(4), 1149–1157. [12] Wells (2000). At home with nature: effects of "greenness" on children's cognitive functioning. Environ Behav, 32(6), 775–795. [13] Barto et al. (2015). How does psychological restoration work in children? An exploratory study. J Child Adolesc Behav 3(3). [14] Faber Taylor et al. (2001). Coping with ADD: The surprising connection to green play settings. Environ Behav, 33(1), 54–77. [15] Amoly et al. (2014). Green and blue spaces and behavioral development in Barcelona schoolchildren: The BREATHE Project. Environ Health Perspect, 122(12)1351–1358. [16] Blair (2009) The child in the garden: An evaluative review of the benefits of school gardening. J Environ Educ, 40(2), 15–38. [17] Rios & Brewer (2014). Outdoor education and science achievement. Appl Environ Educ Commun, 13(4), 234–240. [18] Bell & Dyment (2008). Grounds for health: The intersection of green school grounds and health-promoting schools. Environ Educ Res, 14(1), 77–90. [19] Nedovic & Morrissey (2013). Calm, active and focused: Children's responses to an organic outdoor learning environment. Learn Environ Res, 16(2), 281–295. [20] Ruiz-Gallardo & Valdés (2013). Garden-based learning: An experience with "at risk" secondary education students. J Environ Educ, 44(4), 252–270.

C&NN recognizes that not all studies support causal statements.   ©2016 CHILDREN & NATURE NETWORK

Source: Reprinted from Children & Nature Network. www.childrenandnature.org Used with permission.

To read a QR code, you must have a smartphone or tablet with a camera. We recommend that you download a QR code reader app that is made specifically for your phone or tablet brand.

Source: iStock.com/dolgachov

Balancing Screen Time With Green Time

Despite the mounds of research showing the benefits of green time, we spend most of our lives indoors. A survey of people in 14 countries across Europe and North America reports that on average, people in these countries spend 90% of their time indoors (Velux, 2018). As we are spending more time on screens at school and at home, the amount of time spent outdoors is dwindling. Children ages 8 to 12 spend 4 to 6 hours a day watching or using screens and teenagers average 9 hours a day (AACAP, 2020). Overuse of screens is associated with impaired emotional and social intelligence, technology addiction, social isolation, impaired brain development, and disrupted sleep (Small et al., 2020). On the other hand, moderate screen time for young people can have its benefits, for example, staying in touch with faraway friends and family, researching for a project, answering a question in seconds, organizing tasks, capturing photos, being entertained, having their favorite music at their fingertips, connecting with like-minded individuals all over the world, and the list goes on. Researchers are testing out a digital Goldilocks hypothesis to see if there is an amount of screen time that is "just right," claiming that, "it might be that 'too little' tech use deprives young people of important social information and peer pursuits, whereas 'too much' may displace other meaningful activities" (Przybylski & Weinstein, 2017, p. 2). Balancing screen time with green time might serve as an antidote to some of the negative effects of screen overuse. Researchers studying the psychological effects of screen time and green time concluded, "Nature may currently be an under-utilised public health resource, and it could potentially function as an upstream preventative and psychological well-being promotion intervention for children and adolescents in a high-tech era" (Oswald et al., 2020). Simply put by author Richard Louv, "The more high-tech we become, the more nature we need" (Louv, 2011).

This book provides practical, easy-to-implement strategies for adding time in nature into the school day. Students, teachers, administrators, custodians, support staff, ... *everyone* in your school can benefit from green spaces and green time. By working regular green time into the school day, we can help students develop a lifelong strategy for taking green time to improve their overall wellness and foster lasting connections with nature.

Green Time for All

The research-based benefits of green time summarized in this chapter apply to diverse groups of students and teachers, as well as diverse settings. However, it is important to be aware that the accessibility to green spaces in often not equitable, some students may have negative associations with the outdoors, and others may not feel welcome. For example, children from communities of color and low-income communities tend to have less access to quality natural environments, experiences, and programming (Jennings et al., 2016; Park et al., 2021; Rigolon, 2017). A report from the Center for American Progress details these disparities, stating, "Communities of color are three times more likely than white communities to live in nature deprived places," and "Seventy percent of low-income communities across the country live in nature-deprived areas" (Rowland-Shea et al., 2020). But lack of access is not the only factor; racial discrimination, inequitable park programming, and the feeling of being unwelcome or unsafe can also affect the use of public green spaces by people of color (Byrne, 2012). In response to these issues, the organization

Cities Connecting Children to Nature (CCCN) has chosen equity as their central goal since 2014. CCCN identifies six key principles to increase opportunities for children of color to have access and experiences in nature. Whether you are designing something as large as an outdoor classroom program or as small as a simple pollinator garden, considering these six principles can help you make your space or program more equitable and inclusive.

Source: iStock.com/kali9

Here are six key principles to increase opportunities for children of color to gain more regular access to and experiences in nature. Principles require a commitment to continuous practice and dedication.

- **Recognition and Disruption of Racism:** Continuously acknowledge, recognize, analyze, and interrupt institutional racism and its effects on residents.

- **Culturally Diverse Connections With Nature:** Recognize the many ways diverse cultures, ethnicities, and immigrant groups meaningfully connect with nature.

- **Leadership Opportunities for Youth & Residents:** Provide leadership opportunities for youth and residents in the design and use of natural spaces.

bit.ly/41SPApl

- **Data on Race & Ethnicity:** Regularly collect and use data broken down by race and ethnicity to reflect on progress.
- **Recruitment & Hiring People of Color:** Expand networks and shift recruitment and hiring practices to help people of color join nature-facing professions and city core teams.
- **Equity Outcomes In Policies, Practices, & Investments:** Prioritize equity outcomes when implementing policies, practices, strategic investments, and relationship-building steps.

Source: Advancing Equity in Children's Connection to Nature, CCCN, 2022. Used with permission.

Scan the QR code at the top of this page to access the full resource.

bit.ly/3LtmBDg

Another helpful resource is Children & Nature Network's guide *Anti-Racism and the Outdoors: Resources Related to Inclusion, Diversity, Equity, & Access.* Scan the second QR code on this page to access this resource.

This resource guide includes organizations, presentations, podcasts, affinity groups, books, articles, reports, general anti-racism resources, and ways to be an effective ally.

Source: iStock.com/DenKuvaiev

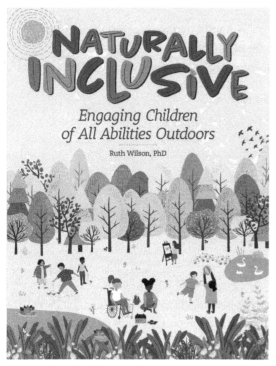

Source: Wilson, R. (2022). *Naturally inclusive: Engaging children of all abilities outdoors.* Gryphon House. Used with permission.

Likewise, students with disabilities may have limited experience with outdoor learning or find outdoor spaces uninviting. It is important to implement necessary adaptations to make green time accessible for students of all abilities. These adaptations might include physical modifications such as paved paths for students who use wheelchairs, special seating that offers support for students with balance issues, or signage for students with hearing impairments. It is also important to consider inclusive modifications to activities based on your students' needs. A helpful resource for creating inclusive outdoor areas and experiences is the book *Naturally Inclusive: Engaging Children of All Abilities Outdoors* (Wilson, 2022). It is a comprehensive guide to making outdoor learning accessible to children of differing abilities and is "based on the knowledge that nature is home to us all and that everyone belongs" (p. 161). The book contains practical guidelines, stories and testimonials from educators, families, and therapists, as well as relevant and recent research around the benefits of nature for children with special needs.

The author, Dr. Ruth Wilson, provides the following examples of how to adapt outdoor learning activities for students of differing abilities in a way that focuses on children's strengths and interests:

For children with social, emotional, and behavioral challenges:
- Provide extra structure for activities and use of materials, such as a defined physical space for activities and boundaries for use of materials, such as a tray for manipulating loose parts.
- Allow reluctant children to observe group activities until they are ready to participate.
- Schedule calming activities after vigorous play.
- Provide extra support during transition times.

For children with hearing impairments:

- Provide visual clues, such as pictures and gestures.
- Combine demonstrations with verbal instructions.
- Stay in the child's visual field.
- Be mindful of the fact that hearing aids amplify not only wanted sounds, such as speech information, but also environmental noise.

For children with visual impairments:

- Provide more tactile and auditory experiences.
- Use hand-over-hand guidance when necessary.
- Place materials at the child's level.
- Provide boundaries, such as trays, boxes, and baskets, for loose materials.

For children with sensory and/or anxiety issues:

- Bring a bucket of snow indoors, if playing with snow outdoors seems overwhelming.
- Keep animals in enclosed structures, such as a tank or cage for fish, birds, or turtles, for observation.
- Watch for signs of discomfort, especially in cold, hot, or rainy weather.

For children with motor difficulties:

- Provide sufficient space for maneuvering a wheelchair and other special equipment.
- Provide elevated work areas.
- Use bolsters for floor activities.
- Provide adaptive seating, as needed.
- Allow extra time for completing tasks.
- Provide larger wheels on walkers and wheelchairs for navigating sand, grass, and other bumpy or soft terrain.
- Always ask a child before providing assistance.

For children with developmental delays:

- Keep directions and explanations simple, organized, and sequenced.
- Break down tasks and other activities into simple steps.

Source: Reprinted from Wilson, R. (2022). *Naturally inclusive: Engaging children of all abilities outdoors* (pp. 23–24). Gryphon House. Used with permission.

https://www
.greenschoolyards
.org/inclusive-design

And of course, work closely with special educators, therapists, parents, and the students themselves to provide any unique adaptations or accommodations that will help individuals experience the most benefit from their time outdoors.

For considerations and strategies for designing inclusive green spaces, scan the QR code at the top of this page to see the Green Schoolyards America webpage on inclusive design. This site provides information on ensuring access, engaging parents and caregivers, engaging district personnel, legal considerations, and strategies to meet the needs of students with specific disabilities.

https://www
.humancentered
design.org/

Another resource that can be helpful as you are designing inclusive outdoor learning areas, or adapting current areas for accessibility and inclusivity, is the Inclusive Design Principles from the Institute for Human Centered Design. These seven principles can help you design or modify outdoor learning areas to make the space more accessible to all learners and educators. For more information on human-centered design, scan the second QR code on this page to see the Institute for Human Centered Design website.

ACKNOWLEDGING INDIGENOUS HISTORY AND PERSPECTIVES

https://native-land.ca/

Another important part of inclusion in outdoor learning is to acknowledge the history of the land you are on. The Native Land app can help you and your students learn about the indigenous peoples who lived on the land that is now your schoolyard, the languages they spoke, and information about their culture. Scan the third QR code on this page to access the app.

A great resource for acknowledging and appreciating the identities of our native students is the Redbud Resource Group's guide titled, *Seeing Our Native Students: A Guide for Educators,* which can be downloaded by scanning the final QR code on this page.

bit.ly/3AmU385

This comprehensive guide includes helpful suggestions to support Native students and educate non-native students. For example, it is important to consider specific communities when teaching about Native peoples, as opposed to grouping all Native peoples together (Redbud Resource Group, 2020). We must educate ourselves about history of Native communities even if we are not history teachers. Our understanding of the historical, environmental, cultural, and psychological aspects of Native history has the potential to help our Native students feel seen, validated, and empowered. A wonderful resource for bringing indigenous perspectives to light is the book, *Braiding Sweetgrass: Indigenous Wisdom, Scientific Knowledge, and the Teachings of Plants,* by Robin Wall Kimmerer, a Potawatomi woman, botanist, and professor of plant ecology.

In this book, Kimmerer shares how considering traditional perspectives and practices of Native Americans can help us make the Earth a better place for future generations. A young adult adaptation of the book was released in 2022, co-written by Monique Gray Smith, a Cree, Lakota, and Scottish woman, and beautifully illustrated by Nicole Neidhardt, a Diné (Navajo) artist of Kiiyaa'áanii clan.

https://www
.outsidevoicespodcast
.com/

Another great resource is the Outside Voices Podcast, which features personal stories about relationships with nature from Black, Indigenous, and People of Color (BIPOC); people with disabilities; and others who are redefining what it means to be "outdoorsy." Scan the QR code on this page to access this resource.

The benefits of green time are plentiful and apply to all of us, but issues with access, attitudes, and prior experiences can get in the way. School is the perfect place to break down these barriers and welcome ALL students into a connection with the natural world. A 2019 review of literature looking at how experiences in nature affect learning states, "It is time to take nature seriously as a resource for learning and development. It is time to bring nature and nature-based pedagogy into formal education—to expand existing, isolated efforts into increasingly mainstream practices" (Kuo et al., p. 6). One way to get started adding nature time to your school day is to incorporate some green breaks and see how they affect your students and you. The next section provides 25 green breaks that can be incorporated into the school day no matter what grade or subject you teach.

References

AACAP (American Academy of Child and Adolescent Psychiatry). (2020). *Screen time and children.* Facts for Families: No. 54. Retrieved February 9, 2023, from https://www.aacap.org/AACAP/Families_and_Youth/Facts_for_Families/FFF-Guide/Children-And-Watching-TV-054.aspx

Amicone, G., Petrucelli, I., De Dominicis, S., Gherardinin, A., Costantino, V., Perucchini, P., & Bonaiuto, M. (2018). Green breaks: The restorative effect of the school environment's green areas on children's cognitive performance. *Frontiers in Psychology, 9,* Article 1579.

Amoly, E., Dadvand, P., Forns, J., López-Vicente, M., Basagaña, X., Julvez, J., Alvarez-Pedrerol, M., Nieuwenhuijsen, M. J., & Sunyer, J. (2014). Green and blue spaces and behavioral development in Barcelona schoolchildren: The BREATHE project. *Environmental Health Perspectives, 122*(12), 1–34.

Anderson, C. L., Monroy, M., & Keltner, D. (2018). Awe in nature heals: Evidence from military veterans, at-risk youth, and college students. *Emotion, 18*(8), 1195–1202.

Bray, I., Reece, R., Sinnett, D., Martin, F., & Hayward R. (2022). Exploring the role of exposure to green and blue spaces in preventing anxiety and depression among young people aged 14–24 years living in urban settings: A systematic review and conceptual framework. *Environmental Research, 214*(Pt 4), 114081.

Byrne, J. (2012). When green is white: The cultural politics of race, nature and social exclusion in a Los Angeles urban national park. *Goeforum, 43*(3), 595–611.

Charles, C., Keenleyside, K., & Chapple, R. (2018). *Home to us all: How connecting with nature helps us care for ourselves and the Earth.* Children & Nature Network.

Chawla, L. (2020). Childhood nature connection and constructive hope: A review of research on connecting with nature and coping with environmental loss. *People and Nature, 2,* 619–642.

Di Carmine, F., & Berto, R. (2020). Contact with Nature can help ADHD children to cope with their symptoms. The state of the evidence and future directions for research. *Visions for Sustainability, 15,* 24–34.

Ernst, J., McAllister, K., Siklander, P., & Storli, R. (2021). Contributions to sustainability through young children's nature play: A systematic review. *Sustainability, 13,* 1–36.

Fägerstam, E., & Blom, J. (2013). Learning biology and mathematics outdoors: Effects and attitudes in a Swedish high school context. *Journal of Adventure Education and Outdoor Learning, 13*(1), 56–75.

French, A. N., Ashby, R. S., Morgan, I. G., & Rose, K. A. (2013). Time outdoors and the prevention of myopia. *Experimental Eye Research, 114,* 58–68.

Frumkin, H., Bratman, G. N., Breslow, S. J., Cochran, B., Kahn, P. H., Jr., Lawler, J. J., Levin, P. S., Tandon, P. S., Varanasi, U., Wolf, K. L., Wood, S. A. (2017). Nature contact and human health: A research agenda. *Environmental Health Perspectives, 125*(7), Article 075001.

Hunter, M. C., Gillespie, B. W., & Chen, S. Y. P. (2019). Urban nature experiences reduce stress in the context of daily life based on salivary biomarkers. *Frontiers in Psychology, 10,* Article 722.

James, J. K., & Williams, T. (2017). School-based experiential outdoor education—A neglected necessity. *Journal of Experiential Education, 40*(1), 58–71.

Jennings, V., Larson, L., & Yun, J. (2016). Advancing sustainability through urban green space: Cultural ecosystem services, equity, and social determinants of health. *International Journal of Environmental Research and Public Health, 13*(2), 196.

Johnstone, A., Martin, A., Cordovil, R., Fjørtoft, I., Iivonen, S., Jidovtseff, B., Lopes, F., Reilly, J. J., Thomson, H., Wells, V., & McCrorie, P. (2022). Nature-based early childhood education and children's social, emotional and cognitive development: A mixed-methods systematic review. *International Journal of Environmental Research and Public Health, 19*, 5967.

Kaplan, R., & Kaplan, S. (1989). *The experience of nature: A psychological perspective.* Cambridge University Press.

Kimmerer, R. W. (2013). *Braiding sweetgrass: Indigenous wisdom, scientific knowledge, and the teachings of plants.* Milkweed Editions.

Kimmerer, R. W., & Smith, M. G. (2022). *Braiding sweetgrass for young adults: Indigenous wisdom, scientific knowledge, and the teachings of plants.* Lerner Publishing.

Kuo, M., Barnes, M., & Jordan, C. (2019). Do experiences with nature promote learning? Converging evidence of a cause-and-effect relationship. *Frontiers in Psychology, 10*, Article 305.

Kuo, M., Browning, H. E. M., & Penner, M. (2018). Do lessons in nature boost subsequent classroom engagement? Refueling students in flight. *Frontiers in Psychology, 8*, Article 2253.

Louv, R. (2012). *The nature principle: Reconnecting with life in a virtual age.* Algonquin Books.

Moula, Z., Palmer, K., & Walshe, N. (2022). A systematic review of arts-based interventions delivered to children and young people in nature or outdoor spaces: Impact on nature connectedness, health and wellbeing. *Frontiers in Psychology, 13*, Article 858781.

Neill, C., Gerard, J., & Arbuthnott, K. D. (2019). Nature contact and mood benefits: Contact duration and mood type. *Journal of Positive Psychology, 14*(6), 756–767.

Oswald, T. K., Rumbold, A. R., Kedzior, S. G. E., & Moore, V. M. (2020). Psychological impacts of "screen time" and "green time" for children and adolescents: A systematic scoping review. *PLOS ONE, 15*(9), 1–52.

Park, K., Rigolon, A., Choi, D., Lyons, T., & Brewer, S. (2021). Transit to parks: An environmental justice study of transit access to large parks in the U.S. West. *Urban Forestry & Urban Greening, 60*, 127055.

Parry, B. J., Thompson, J. L., Holland, M. J. G., & Cumming, J. (2021). Promoting personal growth in young people experiencing homelessness through an outdoor-based program. *Journal of Youth Development, 16*(5), 157–192.

Przybylski, A. K., & Weinstein, N. (2017). A large-scale test of the Goldilocks hypothesis: Quantifying the relations between digital-screen use and the mental well-being of adolescents. *Psychological Science, 28*(2), 204–215.

Redbud Resource Group (RRG). (2020). *Seeing our Native students: A guide for educators.* https://www.redbudresourcegroup.org/seeingournativestudents

Richardson, M., Hallam, J., & Lumber, R. (2015). One thousand good things in nature: Aspects of nearby nature associated with improved connection to nature. *Environmental Values, 24*(5), 603–619.

Rigolon, A. (2017). Parks and young people: An environmental justice study of park proximity, acreage, and quality in Denver, Colorado. *Landscape and Urban Planning, 165,* 73–83.

Rowland-Shea, J, Doshi, S., Edberg, S., & Fanger, R. (2020, July 21). *The nature gap: Confronting racial and economic disparities in the destruction and protection of nature in America.* Center for American Progress. https://www.americanprogress.org/article/the-nature-gap/

Ruiz-Gallardo, J. R., Verde A., & Valdés, A. (2013). Garden-based learning: An experience with "at risk" secondary education students. *Journal of Environmental Education, 44*(4), 252–270.

Taylor, A. F., & Kuo, F. E. (2009). Children with attention deficits concentrate better after walk in the park. *Journal of Attention Disorders, 12*(5), 402–409.

Touloumakos, A. K., & Barrable, A. (2020). Adverse childhood experiences: The protective and therapeutic potential of nature. *Frontiers in Psychology, 11,* 1–9.

Uhls, Y., Michikyan, M., Morris, J., Garcia, D., Small, G., Zgourou, E., Greenfield, P. (2014). Five days at outdoor education camp without screens improves preteen skills with nonverbal emotion cues. *Computers in Human Behavior, 39,* 387–392.

Velux. (2018). *The Indoor Generation Survey: The effects of modern indoor living on health, wellbeing, and productivity.* Retrieved February 8, 2023, from https://press.velux.com/download/542967/theindoor-generationsurvey14may2018-2.pdf

Williams, D. R., & Dixon, P. S. (2013). Impact of garden-based learning on academic outcomes in schools: Synthesis of research between 1990 and 2010. *Review of Educational Research, 83*(2), 211–235.

Wilson, R. (2022). *Naturally inclusive: Engaging children of all abilities outdoors.* Gryphon House.

Xiong, S., Sankaridurg, P., Naduvilath, T., Zang, J., Zou, H., Zhu, J., Lv, M., He, X., & Xu, X. (2017). Time spent in outdoor activities in relation to myopia prevention and control: A meta-analysis and systematic review. *Acta Ophthalmologica, 95*(6), 551–566.

SECTION II

GREEN BREAKS

2 WHAT IS A GREEN BREAK?

As highlighted in Chapter 1, it does not take a long period of time in nature to experience its benefits. A short green break can help your students reset their minds, calm down, lower their stress, and renew their focus. In the context of this book, a green break is a 10- to 20-minute break with the purpose of being immersed in nature. Green breaks can be used at any grade level and in any subject.

Attention Restoration Theory

The green breaks provided in the following chapter are based on attention restoration theory (ART) (Kaplan & Kaplan, 1989), which suggests that the ability to keep our attention on one task is limited and can result in "directed attention fatigue," but attention can be renewed by immersing ourselves in restorative settings. ART identifies four key components to a restorative setting: being away, soft fascination, extent, and compatibility.

KEY COMPONENTS OF A RESTORATIVE SETTING

1. **Being away**—detaching from the environment that is exhausting your attention

2. **Soft fascination**—engaging in activities that hold your attention effortlessly

3. **Extent**—being in an environment in which you feel fully immersed

4. **Compatibility**—feeling that you are in a place that you want to be

Source: iStock.com/Maria Korneeva

Natural environments inherently meet the four requirements for restorative environments. Going outdoors physically *takes you away* from the activities that are causing attention fatigue. Nature provides countless phenomena that *capture your attention effortlessly*, for example, clouds rolling by, green plants, interesting rocks, and so on. Natural settings engage all of your senses resulting in *full immersion* in that space. Compatibility, though, can be a tricky one. Based on different backgrounds and experiences, some people might not be instinctively comfortable in natural environments. *Familiarity fosters compatibility*, so it might take some time for your students to develop familiarity with the green spaces around your school to benefit from this characteristic of a restorative environment.

It is important to note that green breaks are not a substitute for recess. Young students need recess to run, jump, yell, and play, and I would never recommend taking time away from scheduled recess.

Connections to Curriculum

For each green break shared on the following pages, you will see a connections box that includes some ideas for connecting nature to K–12 curriculum. My hope is that these ideas will inspire you to connect nature with the subject(s) you teach. However, it is important to understand that *the green break itself, without connections to curriculum, is worthwhile on its own.* I originally planned to place these connections in another part of the book to stress that the green break alone is enough, but in the end, I decided to include them here as a quick reference for you to extend engagement with the featured natural phenomenon if appropriate. You will also see some resources listed for each green break. Many of these are online resources, all of which were functional at the time of publication. I purposely tried to select websites that would stand the test of time, from organizations like PBS, NOAA, U.S. Fish & Wildlife, NASA, Smithsonian, etc., but I do apologize if any of the URLs are no longer functional by the time you get this book.

Getting Ready for Green Breaks

Below are some things you can do ahead of time to make the most of green breaks for you and your students.

- **Let Students in on the "Why."** When introducing green breaks to your students, share the reason you are implementing green breaks, for example, that scientific research shows time in nature is beneficial to our mental and physical health and can help reset our minds and renew our focus.

- **Set Expectations.** Explain that green breaks are different from recess; they are usually quiet and the purpose is to engage with nature.

- **Designate an Area.** Let students know the area they need to stay within during a green break in order to stay safe and in your view. (You may want to mark the area for younger children.)

- **Discuss Stewardship.** Talk to students about how to be stewards of nature by making sure our actions do not harm the environment (e.g., not pulling leaves or bark off of trees, being gentle with insects and worms, making sure we don't leave litter behind).

- **Assign "Seats."** If you want students to be spread out for a green break, you might put towels or carpet squares out beforehand (especially for younger children).

- **Pack a Bag.** You may want to have a designated "green break bag" that you can grab before you head out. The bag should contain a first aid kit and some of the supplies listed in the next section.

GREEN BREAK SUPPLIES

The following items are good to have on hand for green breaks. You may already have some of these things in your classroom. For the rest, you might consider asking your PTA/PTO for funds to purchase these items, have them donated by local businesses (e.g., carpet squares, journals), or apply for a grant.

- [ ] Pencils
- [ ] Colored pencils
- [ ] Crayons
- [ ] Nature journals or drawing paper
- [ ] Clipboards
- [ ] Towels or carpet squares for sitting outside
- [ ] Hand lenses
- [ ] Folding chairs or benches
- [ ] Binoculars

A NOTE ABOUT WEATHER

Source: iStock.com/ferrantraite

You may have heard the expression "There's no bad weather, only bad clothing," which I believe is true ... to an extent. If students are dressed appropriately for the weather, you should be able to go outside most days; however, there are certain situations when you should not go outside, like during a storm. NEVER take students outdoors when there is lightning and thunder. And be sure to check your school policy on taking students outside. For example, if your school decides that it is too cold or too hot for outdoor recess, you should stay in that day. However, if recess is indoors due to rain or snow, but the temperature is not too cold or too hot, you might consider going outside if students have the proper attire. Let students and their families know that you will be going outdoors regularly so students can dress accordingly. You might want to have a few extra boots, umbrellas, warm coats, gloves, hats, and rain jackets handy for students who might forget or not have access to these things.

SAFETY CONSIDERATIONS

- Do a safety assessment of the land before taking students there. Look for any hazards, such as fallen trees, yellow jacket nests, fire ant hills, poisonous plants, or any other dangers possibly present in your area. Invite an expert from a local nature center or parks department to help with this assessment. See U.S. Fish & Wildlife "Don't Touch These Plants" page:

bit.ly/3Zg6aiQ

- Locate any bodies of water on your school property and take proper precautions to keep children safe.

- Tell students they should never eat any plants, leaves, or berries they find because they can be poisonous.

- Check with your school nurse about student allergies and procedures to prevent and treat them before going outdoors.

- Bring any student emergency equipment (e.g., EpiPens) with you whenever you take students outside.

- Keep a first aid kit handy so you can grab it quickly when you head outdoors with students.

- Establish a "buddy system" where pairs or small groups of students stay together to help each other.

- Make sure students have appropriate clothing for the weather.

- Never take students outdoors when there is thunder and lightning.

- Teach students how to identify poison ivy, poison oak, and poison sumac so they can steer clear of these plants. Scan the QR code below for more on identifying these plants.

bit.ly/3HaNARe

  If students happen to come in contact with any of these plants, have them immediately wash their skin with soap and water and contact your school nurse for further assessment and guidance.

- Teach students what to do if they get lost outside.

- Have students wash their hands when they come inside.

Nature Journals

Source: iStock.com/FatCamera

A journal can be a valuable tool for connecting students with nature. The best resource I have found for guiding students through keeping

HOW TO TEACH
NATURE JOURNALING
CURIOSITY • WONDER • ATTENTION

John Muir Laws and Emilie Lygren
Foreword by Amy Tan

INCLUDES
31 FIELD
ACTIVITIES

Source: Used with permission of Heyday, from *How to Teach Nature Journaling: Curiosity, Wonder, Attention.* John Muir Laws and Emilie Lygren (1986); permission conveyed through Copyright Clearance Center, Inc.

bit.ly/3LreUxj

a nature journal is the book *How to Teach Nature Journaling: Curiosity, Wonder, Attention,* by John Muir Laws and Emilie Lygren. Along with beautiful samples of nature journal pages from naturalists and children, the book provides information on how to manage student groups outdoors, instructions on how to teach drawing, questions to ask yourself as you observe nature, meaningful information to record, and ideas for connecting nature journaling to your curriculum. The book is available in paperback and, remarkably, as a free/donation-based download at John Muir Laws's website, accessible by scanning the first QR code on this page.

One of the activities used in *How to Teach Nature Journaling* is titled "I Notice, I Wonder, It Reminds Me Of" (Laws & Lygren, p. 36). The authors use these three prompts so often in the book that they even have an acronym for them: INIWIRMO! You'll see these three prompts in some of the green breaks in this book. These sentence starters invite students to make observations (I notice), ask questions (I wonder) and make connections (This reminds me of), which can make their green breaks more personal and thus more meaningful.

In addition, John Muir Laws's website is chock-full of useful resources, including free lessons, videos, online meet-ups, and workshops for educators. Scan the QR code on the bottom of this page to access the site.

Know That You Are Making a Difference

https://
johnmuirlaws.com/

When writing about these green breaks, my mind kept going back to the poem "For the Students" by writer and outdoor educator, Emilie Lygren. I think this poem encapsulates how even brief moments in nature can make a difference for your students … and for you.

by Emilie Lygren

Sometimes we sit in circles with these questions:

What are you afraid of?
Who are your heroes and why?
What do you do in your free time that really makes you free?
My students answer:
I have no free time. It is all full of homework, then I take care of my little sister.
My hero is my brother because he walks me home so the bullies don't get me.
Sometimes I am afraid my mother will work so hard she will die.

They are ten, maybe eleven.

I cannot follow them home
and fix it so their parents can
stop leaving,
take their books and burdens
for an hour a day
so they can go be children again.

I can listen when they speak.
I can turn their heads towards the sunrise,
then to the dragonflies hatching by the creek.
I can hold their packs while they run shouting
towards an ocean they have never seen.
I can dump the watering can on their heads
on the hottest day of the year.
I can honor their courage, and their joy.

I cannot always change the world they are living into,
but I can change the world we both live in
for the tremor of a moment,
the same way we all can for one another with a
small smile or knowing sigh
and the fierce act of living in the world with an open heart.

Source: From *What We Were Born For*

The next chapter includes 25 green break ideas, brief moments in nature that are designed to help students refresh, reset, and renew. Choose a few that work for your students within your particular teaching situation. After experiencing the benefits of green breaks, you and your students might want to come up with your own. The possibilities are endless.

References

Kaplan, R., & Kaplan, S. (1989). *The experience of nature: A psychological perspective.* Cambridge University Press.

Laws, J. M., & Lygren, E. (2020). *How to teach nature journaling: Curiosity, wonder, attention.* Heyday.

Lygren, E. (2021). *What we were born for.* Blue Light Press, 1st World Publishing.

NOTES

3
GREEN BREAKS (AND GREEN CONNECTIONS)

Safety First: Before taking students outdoors, be sure to do a safety assessment of the area, and follow the safety guidelines on pages 26 and 27.

Green Break #1

Befriend a Tree

Source: iStock.com/LightFieldStudios

Choose a class tree in your schoolyard or playground, or any place your students spend time on a regular basis. Have students give it a name. (My son named the maple tree in our front yard April. Not after the month but after the girl from Teenage Mutant Ninja Turtles. A decade later, we still refer to the tree as April.) Learn all you can about this tree. What kind is it? Does it keep its leaves year-round? Do a leaf rubbing and/or bark rubbing. Visit the tree throughout the seasons and notice the changes it goes through.

CONNECTIONS

- **K–5 Language Arts:** Read *Our Tree Named Steve* (2005) by Alan Zweibel, illustrated by David Catrow. Make text-to-world connections by comparing the tree in the book to your class tree.

- **K–5 Math:** Measure different parts of the tree (width and height of the leaves, circumference of the trunk).

- **9–12 Math:** Use geometry to estimate the height of your tree.

- The Seek app from iNaturalist can help you identify the species of your tree:

bit.ly/3n2TCwy

- Project Learning Tree has an activity to help students use shadows and ratios to determine the height of a tree:

bit.ly/40BHrod

- The University of British Columbia offers a tutorial on how to use trigonometry to determine the height of a tall tree:

bit.ly/41AryzH

Get to Know the Land You're On

Source: iStock.com/shaunl

Enter your school name and address into Google Maps and use the satellite feature to see an overview of your school grounds. Where are the green spaces? Are there any bodies of water? Are there trees? Then, take a walk around your school grounds to see all of these features first-hand. What places would be good for future green breaks?

CONNECTIONS

- **3–5 Social Studies:** Choose one area of the school grounds and have students create maps of that area using colored pencils and crayons. Have them label key features and/or create a key that shows different features of that the area, such as grass, trees, bodies of water, and so on.

- **9–12 Social Studies:** Research the history of the land that is now your school grounds. Use the Native Land app to learn about the indigenous people who lived on your land, their languages, and their history.

RESOURCES

- A good place to begin learning about the history of your school land is the Native Land Digital website:

native-land.ca

- The Native Governance Center offers a helpful Guide to Indigenous Land Acknowledgment:

bit.ly/3n3tYYx

Meet Your Birds

Source: iStock.com/Liz Leyden

Set up several different kinds of bird feeders and with various types of feed outside a window. If you don't have any windows in your classroom, set up a feeder station in a low traffic area (i.e., not on the playground) where students can go outside to observe the feeders. Notice the different types of birds that visit each of the feeders. Print the Cornell Lab of Ornithology's free mini-posters and use them to get to know the names of the birds that regularly visit your feeders.

CONNECTIONS

- **K–12 Engineering:** Challenge students to build a "bird blind" where a few students can hide to watch the birds and not be seen. You can use fabric, tarps, cardboard boxes, etc.

- **3–5 Science:** Ask students, "What makes a bird a bird?" and have them research the qualities of birds that are different from other animals.

- **6–12: Science:** Have students research the relationship between dinosaurs and birds (see Resources). This understanding makes birds even more fascinating!

- **6–12 Art:** Watch artist Jane Kim create the Cornell Lab's Wall of Birds, a 3,000 square feet mural depicting the phenomenal history and diversity of birds. (See Resources.)

RESOURCES

- Cornell Lab downloadable FeederWatch posters:

bit.ly/3oC5tlv

- Cornell Lab "Flap to the Future" game and lesson plans about the relationship between dinosaurs and birds:

bit.ly/3AtKeVR

- Reflecting Nature: Creating the Wall of Birds video (8:27):

bit.ly/41S9gJQ

Write Your Name With Nature

Source: Left image created by Angelynn Warren. Used with permission. Right image created by August Skibbe. Used with permission.

Take students outdoors and challenge them to write their names with natural objects, such as leaves, sticks, blades of grass, stones, and so on. Ask them to think about the shapes of the letters of their names and what objects might be used to form those letters. They can lay the items on the ground to spell out their names or glue them to a folded piece of cardstock to make a nameplate for their desks.

Tip: Stay away from landscaped areas that could be damaged by students removing stones or mulch, and advise students not to pick parts off of living plants or use any animals, like bugs.

CONNECTIONS

- **K–12 SEL:** Have students share the origin and/or meaning of their name or any other interesting information about their name, such as a person in their family that had the same name, whether it is their full name or a nickname, and so on.

- **K–2 Language Arts:** As students learn to write the letters of the alphabet, challenge them to make the letters out of natural objects as well.

- **K–5 Math:** Use natural objects to represent math equations. (See Resources.)

RESOURCES

- The Edmonton & Area Land Trust provides step-by-step instructions for making a nature name sign:

bit.ly/3ox9WpB

- And a similar activity using natural objects to represent mathematical equations:

bit.ly/41EN86b

The Name Game

Go outdoors and find a natural object (e.g., plant, seed, or insect) and ask, "If you were the first person to ever see this, what name would you give it?" Encourage students to take time to consider the color, shape, smell, size, and texture before they decide on a name. For example, the child in the photo above named the object he is holding a "poke-a-nut" because it looks like a nut and has pokey spikes. Later, you can use the Seek app to find the actual name of it. (A "poke-a-nut" is actually the fruit of the sweet gum tree.)

CONNECTIONS

- **K–12 Science and Language Arts:** Have students create an ID card with a drawing of their natural object, the name they gave it, and its actual name.

- **9–12 Science and Language Arts:** Research how new species are officially named (binomial nomenclature). How is the name determined? What language is used and why? For fun, check out some recently discovered species that were named after celebrities, including a millipede named after Taylor Swift! (See Resources.)

RESOURCES

- Scientists estimate that more than 80% of the 8.7 million species on Earth are yet to be named. Find out more from Yale University's Map of Life:

bit.ly/3NdgAvv

- BBC's Discover Wildlife List of Species Named After Celebrities:

bit.ly/3LtIQZH

Green Break #6

Write a Syntu

Source: **Tom Uhlman**

Have students choose an object in nature to feature in a syntu poem. A syntu has a simple five-line format that requires the writer to take the time to observe a natural object using multiple senses. Line 1: The name of a natural object, plant, animal, or place. Line 2: An observation about Line 1 using only one sense. Line 3: A thought or feeling about Line 1. Line 4: Another observation about Line 1 using a different sense. Line 5: Another word for Line 1. Below is an example of a syntu about spiderwebs.

Spiderweb

Near perfect symmetry

Amazing work

Sticky and strong

Trap

CONNECTIONS

- **K–12 Language Arts:** Share age-appropriate poems about nature. There are several high-quality books of nature poetry available for students of all ages. (See Resources.)

- **K–12 Art:** Invite students to include a drawing of the natural object to accompany the syntu poem.

RESOURCES

- Download a printable Syntu Template:

bit.ly/3V4xfmQ

- Recommended Nature Poetry Books
  - *All the Wild Wonders: Poems of Our Earth* (2010), edited by Wendy Cooling, illustrated by Piet Grobler
  - *Black Nature: Four Centuries of African American Nature Poetry* (2009), edited by Camile T. Dungy
  - *Devotions: The Selected Poems* (2020), by Mary Oliver
  - *The Illustrated Emily Dickinson Nature Sketchbook* (2016), illustrated by Tara Lilly
  - *National Geographic Book of Nature Poetry: More Than 200 Poems With Photographs That Float, Zoom, and Bloom!* (2015) edited by J. Patrick Lewis, former U.S. Children's Poet Laureate
  - *Outside Your Window: A First Book of Nature* (2102), by Nicola Davies, illustrated by Mark Hearld

Hula Hoop Observations

Source: iStock.com/PeopleImages

Place hula hoops on the ground to section off small areas for students to observe. (You might borrow them from the physical education teacher.) Give each student a hand lens, and ask them to use them to look closely at the natural area inside the hoop. Students might be surprised to find many small natural things, such as insects, pill bugs, pebbles, seeds, and plants in that small area. We often miss these tiny natural things as we walk through the schoolyard, so it is fun to zero in on just the hula hoop area so we can notice the small wonders.

CONNECTIONS

- **K–2 Science:** Learn how to tell an insect from other invertebrates (hint: count the legs!), as well as the body parts of insects and how they use them.

- **3–5 Science:** Identify some of the invertebrates that are native to your area.

- **6–8 Science:** Learn about the importance of invertebrates to your local ecosystem.

- **9–12 Science:** Investigate phylum Arthropoda, the largest phylum in the animal kingdom, and how these organisms are classified.

RESOURCES

- Check out the Educational Resources on the Xerces Society website, including Scouting Exercises and the BEETLES Activity Guides:

xerces.org/education

- For older students, the Xerces Society publishes *Wings: Essays on Invertebrate Conservation* twice a year. This publication can be downloaded for free:

bit.ly/3LrL63C

Green Break #8

Spiderweb Walk

Source: iStock.com/Лущан Е.

Take your students on a walk to look for spiderwebs. Morning is best because the dew makes the webs easier to see. Prompt them to notice the different shapes of the webs. They might notice that some seem to have a perfect pattern while others look like a tangled mess; others appear flat across the grass or bushes, while others look like funnels. Encourage students to draw one of the webs and complete the prompts *I notice ..., I wonder ..., This reminds me of ....*

CONNECTIONS

- **K–6 Language Arts and Science**: Read my picture book *Next Time You See a Spiderweb* to learn about the different types of spiderwebs and why spiders make them.

- **3–5 Science and Engineering:** Watch a video of a spider making an orb web (see Resources). Then, challenge students to make a model of an orb web in a door frame using masking tape. Hint: They can create a frame and radial threads out of the nonsticky side and use the sticky side to add a capture spiral. Toss some wads of paper into the web to represent flying insects. Do they stick? How is your web similar to a real spiderweb? How is it different?

RESOURCES

- Time-Lapse Video of an Orb-Weaving Spider Making a Web (1:01), from Wonderopolis:

bit.ly/3K1Qtpc

- Beautiful Spider Web Build Time-Lapse (4:36), from BBC Earth:

bit.ly/3ArwOcP

Nature Sketches

Source: istock.com/Image Source

Give each student a clipboard, plain paper (or nature journals), pencil, and something to sit on (towel or carpet square). Invite them to choose something outdoors that they would like to sketch with a pencil. Remind students that a sketch is a rough drawing, so it does not need to be perfect. Encourage them to choose something that they would like to observe more closely. Let students know ahead of time how much time they will have to make their sketches.

CONNECTIONS

- **K–12 Science**: Have students research the natural object they drew. The extent of the research will depend on the age of the students. For kindergarten it might be learning the name and writing it. For high school it could be using the Seek app to identify the species and researching its role in the ecosystem.

RESOURCES

- The Seek app from iNaturalist:

bit.ly/3n2TCwy

- John Muir Laws's blog archives contain hundreds of video tutorials on how to draw objects in nature:

bit.ly/3AtL8Sf

Nature Scavenger Hunt

Source: Tom Uhlman

This green break is perfect for a time when your students need to move around a bit. Take your students outside to a natural area and challenge them to find something in your schoolyard that has a certain trait or quality. For example, you could ask them to find something yellow, or find something soft, or find something symmetrical. To make it a little more complex, you could ask them to find something that has multiple qualities, like yellow, soft, and symmetrical. (I'm thinking dandelion!) If you want each student to search for something different, you can write different adjectives on index cards and hand them out to students. Or you can purchase the gofindit card game (pictured above) that is specially designed for a nature scavenger hunt.

CONNECTIONS

- **K–12 Language Arts:** Create scavenger hunt cards using vocabulary that students are learning in class and see if they can find a natural object that matches the vocabulary word. To enhance this, have students research synonyms for the words on the cards and then decide whether or not those synonyms apply to the natural object they found.

- **6–8 Science:** Send students on a scavenger hunt for biotic (living) and abiotic (non-living) components of your schoolyard. They can list them on a t-chart. Set a time limit and have students compare their lists when they finish.

RESOURCES

- The picture book *Finding Wild* (2016), written by Megan Wagner Lloyd and illustrated by Abigail Halpin, is a great book to share before a nature scavenger hunt.

- Educator Mark Drollinger has a helpful video (2:40) describing the interactions of biotic and abiotic factors in an ecosystem:

bit.ly/3L8K7no

- The gofindit card game (pictured on the previous page):

bit.ly/40DQKUv

Shades of Green

Source: **Tom Uhlman**

Did you know that Crayola crayons makes 49 shades of green? And several of them are named after things in nature: inchworm, fern, shamrock, and pine green to name a few. See which greens are in your crayon box and challenge your students to match each shade of green to something outdoors. You could also get some paint swatches from your local paint store and challenge students to find natural objects that match each color swatch.

CONNECTIONS

- **K–5 Science and Art:** Invite students to make various shades of green from yellow and blue paint. Have them experiment with adding different amounts of each color and compare the results. Maybe have them come up with their favorite shade of green and, in Crayola-style, give it a fun name.

- **6–12 Science:** Learn about chlorophyll (the molecule responsible for the green color in plants) and how its key role in photosynthesis provides the foundation for life on Earth.

- **6–12 Science:** Learn about the physics behind seeing colors and the chemistry of how colors are made. The Smithsonian Libraries "Color in a New Light" website is a great place to start. (See Resources.)

RESOURCES

- See all of Crayola's shades of green and learn more about color at the Crayola website:

crayola.com/explore-colors/

- Smithsonian Libraries Color in a New Light website:

bit.ly/3HfMpAe

Cloud Watch

Source: iStock.com/MediaProduction

Choose a partly cloudy day for this one! Have each student bring a towel outside with them and choose a spot to lie down where the clouds are visible. Give students time to quietly watch the clouds. You might have them sketch the clouds and complete the prompts, *I notice ..., I wonder ..., It reminds me of ...,* and write them in their journals.

Safety Note: Caution students to NEVER look directly at the Sun.

CONNECTIONS

- **3–5 Science:** Learn about the different types of clouds and the kind of weather usually associated with each.

- **9–12 Language Arts and Music:** Choose a song about clouds (there are so many) for students to listen to and analyze the lyrics, such as "Both Sides Now" by Joni Mitchell, "Heavy Cloud No Rain" by Sting, or "Cloud Nine" by the Temptations. Find other examples of how nature and art intersect to share and interpret.

- NASA S'COOL Program has a simple Cloud Identification Chart:

bit.ly/41EJAAE

- The National Weather Service provides a more detailed Cloud Identification Chart:

bit.ly/43svUZS

Shadow Play

Source: iStock.com/prospective56

Take students outdoors in the morning or afternoon (when shadows are longer) and challenge them to make different shapes with their shadows. They can use their hands or bodies, in groups or by themselves. Maybe they can spell a word or make a monster or create an animal. Notice where the Sun is in the sky and the direction of the shadows. You might want to try again at another time of day and compare size and direction of the shadows.

CONNECTIONS

- **K–5 Art and Language Arts:** Create an outdoor shadow play! Use cardstock to cut out various characters and shapes and tape them on popsicle sticks or chopsticks. Students can write a story about the characters and act it out with the shadows of the cut-outs.

- **3–5 Science:** Have students trace each other's shadows with chalk in the morning, noon, and afternoon. Compare the size and direction of the shadows and note where the Sun is in the sky each time.

- **6–12 Art:** Show students some examples of shadows that can be created with your hands and invite them to try it.

RESOURCES

- PBS Learning Media has a video titled *Shifting Shadows* (1:27), which shows students tracing the shadows of various playground equipment on the blacktop and then observing the change in the shadows just minutes later:

bit.ly/3AtMbBO

- Observing Shadows on Earth: PBS LearningMedia has a helpful model that explains why shadows change throughout the day:

bit.ly/40zVw5r

- Blink of an Eye Arts Tool Kit features an art installation designed by artist and professor Erin Taylor at the University of Cincinnati that allows people to create shadows on a screen with their bodies:

bit.ly/3mY40pt

Rock Balancing

Source: iStock.com/sultancicekgil

Collect some rocks from a rocky area outdoors (or bring in some river stones from a local landscaping store if you don't have a rocky area). Rocks that are small enough to fit in the palm of your hand are ideal for this. Introduce students to the activity of rock balancing, which involves stacking rocks on top of each other slowly and thoughtfully to make a stack. Have students experiment with stacking different sizes and shapes to discover what works best. When you are finished, take the rock stacks down so that they don't interfere with the local ecosystem.

CONNECTIONS

- **K–5 Science and Language Arts:** Read *If You Find a Rock* (2008), by Peggy Christian, and invite students to bring in a special rock. Discuss properties of rocks and the uses of different types of rocks.

- **9–12 Social Studies and Science:** Research how different cultures have used stacks of rocks, sometimes called cairns, for different purposes, such as marking a route to food or safety or marking a burial site, as well as concerns about how rock cairns could cause harm to the local ecosystem if not built or placed thoughtfully. (See Resources.)

- National Park Service article on rock cairns in national parks:

bit.ly/3HfMIuS

- Zion National Park, "Balancing Act: The History of Rock Cairns and Why Stacking Rocks Is Discouraged in Zion":

bit.ly/3V2vUgB

NOTES

Green Break #15

Catching Snowflakes

Source: iStock.com/ChaoticMind75

Snowfall is one of the most fascinating weather events we experience here on Earth. People of all ages get excited when it snows. Consider taking your students outdoors the next time it snows to get a closer look at shapes and patterns of water in one of its most beautiful forms. Store some dark construction paper or fabric in the freezer (or set some outside in the cold an hour or so beforehand) so the snowflakes have a cold surface to land and won't melt. When you go outside, give each student a small piece of the cold paper to catch some snowflakes and a hand lens to take a closer look. Discuss the shapes and patterns they see. Hint: Usually, the closer the temperature is to 32 degrees F, the larger the snowflakes will be, and the colder it is, the smaller the snowflakes will be.

CONNECTIONS

- **K–5 Language Arts and Science:** Read *Curious About Snow* (2016) by Gina Shaw to learn about how snow forms, why snow is white, as well as the reason for the six-sided pattern of snowflakes.

- **6–12 Science and Art:** Explore *The Secret Life of a Snowflake: An Up-Close Look at the Art and Science of Snowflakes* (2010) by scientist Kenneth Libbrecht to see photos of snowflakes taken with a microscope and in-depth explanations of how snowflakes form in a six-sided pattern.

- **9–12 Chemistry:** Learn how the structure of water molecules results in the six-sided shape of snowflakes. The TED-Ed video "The Science of Snowflakes" shares a great visual explanation of this fascinating phenomenon. (See Resources.)

RESOURCES

- NOAA's webpage titled "How Do Snowflakes Form? Get the Science Behind Snow" includes a Q&A about how snowflakes form and some microscopic photos of snowflakes:

bit.ly/40lfM4W

- The TED-Ed video *The Science of Snowflakes* (4:29) can be found here:

bit.ly/41ZsqNU

Leaf Rubbing

Source: Tom Uhlman

This activity is best done in the fall when leaves are on the ground. Before you take students outside, demonstrate how to do a leaf rubbing by placing a tree leaf upside down on a hard surface (like a clipboard), placing a piece of paper over it, and gently rubbing a crayon on the paper to reveal the shape and pattern of the leaf. Then, take students outside to collect some tree leaves and make their own leaf rubbings. Invite students to compare the shapes and sizes of the leaves and the patterns the lines in the leaves create.

Be sure to tell students to collect fallen leaves from the ground and not to pick them off of the trees.

bit.ly/3HaNARe

Safety Note: Make sure students know how to identify poison ivy, poison sumac, and poison oak before collecting leaves. Scan the QR code on this page for information on identifying these plants.

CONNECTIONS

- **K–2 Language Arts and Art**: Read *Leaf Man* (2005) by Lois Ehlert and invite students to make their own pictures out of leaves or leaf rubbings and create stories to go along with their pictures.

- **3–5 Science:** Research why leaves change color and why some trees do not lose their leaves.

- **6–12 Science:** Use the Arbor Day "What Tree?" online key to figure out what tree your leaf came from. (See Resources.)

RESOURCES

- Why Do Leaves Change Color SciJinks Lesson from NOAA:

bit.ly/3NdgbZX

- *Why Do Leaves Change Color? A Let's-Read-And-Find-Out Science book* (2015) by Betsy Maestro, illustrated by Loretta Krupinski

- Arbor Day "What Tree Is That?" online key:

bit.ly/40zWxKN

Symmetry Search

Source: iStock.com/Elena Abrosimova

Take students outdoors to look for things in nature that have the quality of being symmetrical, put simply, that one half is the mirror image of the other half. Students will likely notice that nature is full of symmetry—in flowers, insects, leaves, even themselves. Invite them to draw or photograph some of the symmetrical natural objects they find. You could also have them look for some objects that are asymmetrical to compare.

CONNECTIONS

- **K–2 Art:** Create symmetrical butterfly paintings. (See Resources.)

- **3–8 Math:** Learn about different types of symmetry (e.g. radial symmetry, bilateral symmetry, near symmetry, and asymmetry) and look for examples from nature.

- **11–12 Science and Math:** Oxford University recently (March 2022) released a paper proposing an explanation for why so many objects in nature are symmetrical. (See Resources.)

RESOURCES

- Maine Audubon Instructional video (2:44) for making symmetrical butterfly paintings with young children:

bit.ly/44rBlth

- "Nature Prefers Symmetry and Simplicity" from Oxford University:

bit.ly/3NlbtJE

Looking for Shapes

Source: Tom Uhlman

Take students outside to look for shapes in nature: squares, triangles, circles, cubes, prisms, cylinders, spheres, and so on. Invite them to draw or photograph natural objects and label their shapes. Older students can look for fractals, non-geometric shapes that repeat in a pattern, such as tree branches, or the Fibonacci sequence in natural objects, such as flower petals or pinecone seed pods. (See Resources for more examples.)

CONNECTIONS

- **K–5 Math:** Look for the geometric shapes that students are learning in class. You may want to focus on just one shape at a time for younger students.

- **6–8 Math:** Learn about fractals, non-geometric shapes that repeat in a pattern, and how to identify them in nature.

- **9–12 Math:** Introduce students to the Fibonacci sequence and look for examples outdoors in your area.

- **K–12 Art:** Introduce students to the work of artist Charley Harper, who used simple shapes and lines to create representations of animals and plants. Younger students can recognize the simple geometric shapes used in Harper's work, and older students can appreciate the challenge of representing the organic shapes of plants and animals in such a minimalist geometric way.

- Examples of Charley Harper's work, prints, and books for children and adults that feature his artwork can be found at charleyharperartstudio.com:

charleyharperartstudio.com

- The Carnegie Museum of Natural History's webpage titled Math in Nature? It All Adds Up! provides an overview of the Fibonacci sequence and common shapes that are found in nature:

bit.ly/41BqBXD

- The book *Mysterious Patterns: Finding Fractals in Nature* (2014) by Sarah C. Campbell uses photographs and simple language to explain what fractals are and how to identify them in nature.

- The book *Growing Patterns: Fibonacci Numbers in Nature* (2010) by Sarah C. Campbell provides a simple, illustrated explanation of the Fibonacci sequence.

Plant Something and Watch It Grow

Source: Photo by Julie Singer. Used with permission.

This activity can involve something as simple as planting seeds in a pot to something as complex as designing and installing a vegetable or pollinator garden. Either way, getting students' hands in the dirt, planting, watering, and caring for plants can provide a meaningful connection with nature. Involve students in researching the plants and their needs before planting. Going outside to check on and care for plants makes a great green break.

CONNECTIONS

- **K–2 Science:** Learn about the basic needs of plants, and compare them to the basic needs of animals.

- **3–5 Science:** Learn about the importance of pollinators and what can be done to help them thrive in your area.

- **6–12 Science:** Research native plants in your area and how native plantings can help the wildlife in your local ecosystem.

RESOURCES

- Audubon has a Native Plant Database where you can enter your zip code to find a list of plants native to your area:

bit.ly/3AraaRW

- The National Wildlife Federation has a search tool for finding native plants in your area:

bit.ly/3Nd8yTh

- U.S. Fish and Wildlife offers a guide for planning and planting a pollinator garden:

bit.ly/40GwZvD

- The Xerces Society's "Bring Back the Pollinators" program provides helpful information on pollinators and offers a way to register your pollinator garden with them:

bit.ly/3L8DH7L

Watching the Wind

Source: iStock.com/Antonio_Diaz

A day with a slight breeze is best for this activity. Give each student a bubble wand and a small cup of bubble solution. They can use bubbles to observe the wind by blowing a single bubble and watching it be carried away until it finally pops. They can do this over and over again, watching where bubbles go, counting the seconds until they pop, or even blowing multiple bubbles at once to see how the wind spreads them out.

CONNECTIONS

- **K–2 Science:** Experiment with different shaped bubble wands (you can make them out of pipe cleaners) to see if the shape of the wand affects the shape of the bubble. Then, read *Pop! A Book About Bubbles* (2001) by Kimberly Brubaker Bradley to learn why free-floating bubbles are always round.

- **3–8 Science:** Have students make their own bubble solution by using different amounts of three main ingredients: dish soap, glycerin, and water. (See Resources.)

- **9–12 Science and Language Arts:** Learn different literary words used to describe wind (e.g., sirocco, Aeolian, gale, zephyr, wuther, squall, haboob), and challenge students to use these words in their writing and/or in conversation when describing the wind on a particular day. (See Resources.)

RESOURCES

- Check out Merriam-Webster's Wordplay website for 7 Names for Different Types of Wind:

bit.ly/3oKJ9pQ

- PBS offers instructions for making really big bubbles as well as a few different recipes for homemade bubble solution:

bit.ly/43Xmkjb

Kaleidoscopes

Source: **Tom Uhlman**

Looking through a kaleidoscope can serve as great brain break, and using them in nature can make the break even more immersive. Have students experiment by looking at different natural objects with kaleidoscopes. Ask them which natural objects are most interesting to look at through a kaleidoscope and why. The Resources section below includes a variety of kaleidoscopes that can be used with natural objects.

Safety Note: Warn students not to look at the Sun in their kaleidoscope.

CONNECTIONS

- **3–5 Science and Engineering:** Learn how light and a certain configuration of mirrors make kaleidoscopes work, and then try to make your own.

- **9–12 History and Art:** Research the history of the kaleidoscope, its inventor, mathematician and physicist Sir David Brewster, and the "Kaleidoscope Craze" of 19th-century England.

- For younger students, Fun Express Plastic Prisms can be aimed at natural objects to create interesting patterns for the viewer:

bit.ly/3mY8FHZ

- And the Nature Kaleidoscope is available from Montessori Services:

bit.ly/3H9chNR

- For older students there are DIY wooden kaleidoscopes that can be easily filled with natural objects such as the one pictured on the previous page made by Vidonio:

bit.ly/41ZIIGS

Poem in Your Pocket

Source: iStock.com/Liia Galimzianova

Print out some nature poems small enough that students can fit one in their pocket. You can give each student the same poem or different poems. Distribute the poems, and invite them to bring their poem and a towel or carpet square to sit on outdoors. Provide time for students to read the poems individually. After that, you might invite them to either draw a picture inspired by their poem or to form groups of two or three to discuss the poems using the **I notice ..., I wonder ..., This reminds me of ...** prompts. Allow students to keep their pocket poem to share with others.

CONNECTIONS

- **K–12 Language Arts:** Research the poets from this activity. When were they born, where did they live, what about their life experiences relates to their poem? Are all or most of their poems about nature, or do they write about other things? Be sure to choose poems written by people of different races, ethnicities, ages, life experiences, and time periods.

- **K–12 Music:** Listen to songs (poems set to music) about nature like "What a Wonderful World" by Louis Armstrong, "Birdsong" by the Wailin' Jennys, or "Sunshine on My Shoulders" by John Denver. Print out the lyrics and discuss how the music helps express the meaning of the words.

RESOURCES

- Recommended Nature Poetry Books
  - *All the Wild Wonders: Poems of Our Earth* (2010), edited by Wendy Cooling, illustrated by Piet Grobler
  - *Black Nature: Four Centuries of African American Nature Poetry* (2009), edited by Camile T. Dungy
  - *Devotions: The Selected Poems* (2020), by Mary Oliver
  - *The Illustrated Emily Dickinson Nature Sketchbook* (2016), illustrated by Tara Lilly
  - *National Geographic Book of Nature Poetry: More Than 200 Poems With Photographs That Float, Zoom, and Bloom!* (2015) edited by J. Patrick Lewis, former U.S. Children's Poet Laureate
  - *Outside Your Window: A First Book of Nature* (2012), by Nicola Davies, illustrated by Mark Hearld

- April is National Poetry Month and each year the Academy of American Poets designate a day in April as Poem in Your Pocket Day. For this year's date and more information, go to the Academy of American Poets website:

bit.ly/41GuCdy

Nature Walks

Source: iStock.com/Caiaimage/Paul Bradbury

Take students on a walk outdoors in a natural area. To help students be more mindful on the walk and less distracted by thoughts or worries, choose a focus for the walk each time. For example, you could invite students to center in on just one of their senses throughout the walk, like a Listening Walk. Or make it a seasonal walk where students look for signs of the season, like a Signs of Spring Walk. Or a walk where you look and listen for evidence of animals, like tracks or bird sounds, a Signs of Wildlife Walk.

CONNECTIONS

- **K–5 Science:** Become familiar with your wildlife neighbors. Choose an animal, plant, or fungus that you see on your walk and do some research on it. Then, next time you see it, you'll know more about it.

- **6–12 Science:** Learn about invasive species in your area and their effect on your local ecosystem. Look for these species next time you take a nature walk, and research how these invasive species should be handled.

RESOURCES

- Purdue University 4H at Home has an activity titled "Neighborhood Hunt for Signs of Wildlife" that could be used at school to find evidence of wildlife without even seeing an animal:

bit.ly/46PrMGb

- For younger students, University of Washington offers an activity where students can use their "Owl Eyes," "Deer Ears," "Raccoon Hands," or "Dog Noses" to detect certain things on a nature walk:

bit.ly/3n3AVc5

- The book *Aliens From Earth: When Animals and Plants Invade Other Ecosystems* (2016), written by Mary Batten and illustrated by Beverly Doyle, introduces students to the consequences of introducing invasive species into an ecosystem either accidentally or deliberately.

Nature Stretches

Source: iStock.com/Satoshi-K

Many yoga poses are named after things in nature, like tree pose, mountain pose, cat–cow, downward dog, and the lesser known squirrel pose! Take students outdoors (with towels to use as yoga mats) and teach them a few of these poses. Have students come up with some of their own poses based on natural objects that they choose. For example, what might a grass pose, pill bug pose, or bird pose look like?

CONNECTIONS

- **K–12 Physical Education:** Learn about the fundamental components of yoga practice: postures, breathing, relaxation, and mediation.

- **3–5 Math:** Learn about different types of triangles and create them with your bodies using Triangle Yoga from PBS Learning Media.

RESOURCES

- Greater Good Science Center: "Seven Ways That Yoga Is Good for Schools":

bit.ly/41X4nPP

- Classroom Connection: Triangle Yoga Math 4–5

bit.ly/42g8Q0j

Bring the Outdoors In

Source: iStock.com/janiecbros

Indoor plants are a great way to bring green time into your school. There are many benefits to having live plants in your classroom. (See Resources.) Caring for plants can serve as a nice green break for a student who needs to reset, refocus, or relax for a few minutes. You and all of your students can benefit from the peaceful atmosphere created by the plants all day, every day. If you have very young students who might nibble on plants, be sure to choose plants that are nontoxic.

CONNECTIONS

- **K–5 Science**: Learn about the needs of plants and how to properly care for them.

- **K–5 Math:** Measure your classroom plants as they grow.

- **6–8 Science:** Learn about plant processes, such as photosynthesis and respiration.

- **9–12 Science:** Learn how different kinds of plants reproduce—seeds, spores, and vegetative propagation (e.g., bulbs, corms, tubers, rhizomes, and stolons).

RESOURCES

- Edutopia offers suggestions for the "10 Best Plants for the Classroom":

bit.ly/41ShAt4

- Edutopia: "5 Reasons to Bring Plants Into the Classroom":

bit.ly/3n5tils

Choose Your Own Green Breaks

After your students have experienced several green breaks, invite them to come up with their own ideas for green breaks that you could take as a class. Make a running list of their green break ideas and try them throughout the school year! Not every student has to be doing the same thing on every green break. You might want to try an open green break where students can choose their own activity from all of the ones you have tried so far. The important thing is taking some time to disconnect from the activities draining attention to connect with nature.

My hope is that as students experience the benefits of green time, they will begin to integrate green breaks into their lives beyond the school day and, eventually, carry this strategy with them throughout their lives.

Those who contemplate the beauty of the earth find
reserves of strength that will endure as long as life lasts.

—Rachel Carson

SECTION III

GREEN EDUCATORS

GREEN TEACHING

4

This chapter features educators who are finding creative ways to bring more green time into the school day in a variety of settings. Their projects might inspire you to be creative with your space, like Ann Troyer who runs a roof-top garden program at a pre-K through sixth-grade inner city school (p. 90); develop a unique partnership, like Kerri Miles, a park employee who facilitates a field trip partnership between the parks department and local school district (p. 88); or create a brand new program, like high school teacher Aaron Parker whose garden program for English language learners has developed into an Agricultural Career Tech Pathway (p. 87).

From writing a grant for a class set of rain boots to transforming an empty lot into a community park, a wide-range of projects are highlighted. My hope is that these stories will provide inspiration for green projects that will enhance your unique teaching situation.

Green Projects

ALL-WEATHER WONDER WALKS

Source: Photo by Sarah Currier. Used with permission.

Kindergarten teacher Sarah Currier takes daily "Wonder Walks" with her students in the green space surrounding their school. Realizing the benefits of this daily green time activity, she wanted to be able to take these walks no matter what the weather. So, she wrote a grant to her local community foundation to provide a class set of rain boots that her students could wear in the rain, snow, and mud. The students were thrilled to have their own set of boots and use carabiner clips to keep their two boots hooked together when not wearing them. Right now, storage is a large cardboard box underneath a table, but the class plans to design their own boot storage system in the future.

Every time we put our boots on and go
outside, it feels like an adventure.

—Harper, Kindergartner

Our boots are the best because they let us
go outside even when it's messy out.

—Lucas, Kindergartner

Some of our greatest memories as a class
involve snow, ice, puddles, and mud.

—Sarah Currier

MORNINGS IN THE GARDEN

Source: Photo by Francesca Gettelman. Used with permission.

Student members of the Eldorado School Garden Club show up early in the morning to tend to their garden. In the spring, summer, and fall, they care for their plants, and in the winter, they research, plan, and work on the rock pathways. Fifth-grade teacher Francesca Gettelman knows that gardening is good for kids and has found creative ways to make this garden a reality at her school. The raised beds were added as part of her daughter's eighth-grade pinnacle project. The PTO helps fund the garden, Francesca brings in gardening tools, and parents help out, too. The garden means a lot to the club members who range from first to fifth grade.

When asked why they show up early to school each day to work on the garden, students replied:

> *I like to see work pay off and it's easy*
> *to see that with a garden.*
>
> —Sam, fifth grader

> *I like how it adds colors and how we get*
> *to see the beautiful flowers.*
>
> —Parker, second grader

> *I'm not a fan of global warming. The little things matter.*
>
> —Greta, fifth grader

LEARNING LANGUAGE THROUGH GARDENING

Source: Photos by Aaron Parker. Used with permission.

Aaron Parker is a teacher of English language learners (ELLs) at Aiken High School who specializes in working with students with limited or interrupted formal education. He has 260 international students from 40 countries, who speak over 50 languages, many of them refugees. Aaron discovered that, for many of his students, gardening provided a connection between the life they lived before and the life they live now, creating a meaningful avenue for language acquisition, vocabulary development, and interaction. So, he started an after-school garden club where his students could share their strengths and expertise, improve their language skills, and take home the harvest to share with their families. Since starting the program 5 years ago, that garden club has grown into an Agricultural Career Tech Pathway available for students who want to pursue a career in agriculture. The community garden space now has 35 raised beds, a covered outdoor classroom, a high tunnel, a greenhouse, and animals that students care for, such as alpaca, quail, goats, ducks, donkeys, a steer, chickens, and rabbits. The program not only provides students rich learning experiences but also fosters a sense of community and belonging for students and their families.

> *Our Aiken agriculture program helped me feel more at home in a foreign country. It has given us (international students) a sense of community and belonging, which is something that is rare to find.*
>
> —Joyeuse, 12th grader

> *Beyond just growing crops, our Aiken agriculture program fosters a community where international students may join together and form friendships that cut over race, gender, culture, and background. Anybody who enters the farm becomes a farmer.*
>
> —Pawan, 11th grader

> *My mother said she likes the farm and the animals because it reminded her of the days when she used to farm in Bhutan. If there's a chance in the future, she wants to purchase a land and continue farming and raising animals.*
>
> —Ankita, 11th grader

SCHOOL AND PARKS PARTNERSHIP

Source: Photo by Maya Merland. Used with permission.

The Kettering City School District and Kettering Parks, Recreation and Cultural Arts Department have developed a unique relationship to engage students in outdoor learning. The school district partners with park staff and provides busing so all K–5 students from its eight elementary schools can experience immersive field trips in the city parks. Classes can come as often as they like to experience nature throughout the seasons. The lessons taught on these trips were written by district elementary teachers and taught by park staff and volunteers—a true partnership.

> *When the students visit our Land Labs, nature becomes the teacher and it is amazing to watch them turn into little naturalists.*
>
> —Kerri Miles,
> Environmental Education Supervisor

Source: Photos by Katie Guirnalda and Saralinda Blanning. Used with permission.

All kindergarten and first-grade students in Centerville City Schools participate in Nature Class each week where they are involved in hands-on lessons about local plants and animals. It started as a Parent-Teacher Organization (PTO) funded experience that employed a "Naturalist in Residency," who shared nature-based learning experiences with students outdoors. The school board was so impressed with the benefits students were experiencing from the program that the class is now funded by the district and is on every kindergartner's and first grader's specials rotation, like art, music, and physical education. There are now two full-time Nature Class teachers at the district's two primary schools, Laura Peterson and Katie Guirnalda. Many partners are involved in this program, including a local nature-based advocate, the park district, parents, and numerous Eagle Scouts who develop natural spaces in both locations that allow for nature-based lessons and nature play.

> For the past 17 years, our young scientists have called me the "nature teacher," but I can assure you that nature is the teacher. I am more of a gatherer of wonderings, thoughts, and ponderings. The children open up their "science tool kit" (their five senses), reflect on the beauty around them, and connect with their natural world. Every child needs and deserves experiences outside in nature.
>
> —Laura Peterson

It has been wonderful being able to teach nature full-time and give so many students an outdoor learning experience! Most nature lessons consist of a hands-on learning activity such as birdwatching, planting or harvesting vegetables, looking for animal tracks, building in the snow, digging for worms and more!

—Katie Guirnalda

ROOFTOP GARDEN

Source: Photos by Julie Singer. Used with permission.

Despite being located in the heart of a bustling city, students at Rothenburg Preparatory Academy have regular access to vibrant gardens filled with vegetables and flowers. They do this through a rooftop garden program run by education coordinator Ann Troyer and volunteer and garden coordinator Julie Singer. Students have garden class every week where they care for various plants and enjoy the harvest in smoothie parties and salad parties. In the summer, older students can apply for paid garden care jobs to keep things going when school is out. This unique and creative program is something you have to see. Check out their website, https://www.rothenbergrooftopgarden.com/. (To see the garden, be sure to view on a computer, not a mobile device.)

Our students get to experience firsthand the joy of harvesting a carrot or radish they started from seed and witness a butterfly or bee visit a flower they planted. Everyone and everything is connected, and our garden helps children see where they fit in.

—Ann Troyer

*The Rothenberg Rooftop Garden provides a safe outdoor
environment where children can experience growing their
own food from start to finish. For most, this is their only
opportunity to garden, and it is heartwarming to see
how excited they get to simply water a plant or sow a
seed. Our time together in the rooftop garden is a brief
and welcome respite from their tech-saturated lives.*

—Julie Singer

*We get to learn about plants and measuring. I like
being outside better than being in the classroom.
Things I like to eat are carrots and lettuce.*

—Komuryi, third grader

OUTDOOR LEARNING CENTER

Source: Photos by David Joy. Used with permission.

Teachers and students in Grades 7 through 9 at Wahlquist Junior
High in West Ogden, Utah, have access to two outdoor classrooms,
six garden beds, a greenhouse, compost area, and shed, thanks to
the vision of Dr. David Joy, an eighth-grade science teacher and
researcher in outdoor education and social justice. With the help
of school administrators, teachers, and maintenance staff, David
has put his research into action by creating this outdoor learning
space for the students of Wahlquist, with special attention to making the space inclusive and open to all. For example, smooth pavers
have been installed to aid accessibility for all students. With funding from the Utah Office of Recreation and Utah State University,

this outdoor area continues to grow with plans for bird boxes, bat boxes, bee houses, and trail cams. David notes that working closely with the school maintenance staff has been essential to the success of these outdoor learning areas.

We are trying to find a way to help ALL of our students get outside and reconnect with nature. They can't learn and care about what they don't know, so we are working to reintroduce them, and it is paying off in a big way.

—Dr. David Joy

STUDENT-DEVELOPED COMMUNITY PARK

Source: Photo by Shane Allison. Used with permission.

School nurse Shane Allison works in Northridge Local Schools, one of the smallest urban districts in the state of Ohio, where students in the community spend very little time outside. He realizes the benefits of green space on students' physical and mental health and has come up with a plan for students to convert the 20+ acre empty lot next to his campus into a community park. Polar Park, named after the high school's Polar Bear mascot, will be half nature park (plants, animals, etc.) and half community park (walking trails, skate park, etc.). Shane has pulled together a network of community partners to form an advisory council for the project that includes local universities and civic organizations, and has developed a program called Community STEM with four new high school courses: Community STEM 1, Community STEM—Natural Resources, Community STEM—Sustainability, and Community STEM—Parks and Rec. Through these courses, students in the Community STEM program are 100% responsible for developing and maintaining Polar Park and programming its activities for the Northridge community. He wants the community to feel ownership of the park and knows that its location right next to the school will allow for student involvement both during and after the school day.

> *Our kids just don't go outside enough. For many,*
> *safety is a concern where they live, so being able to*
> *travel somewhere to connect to nature is unrealistic.*
> *Having 20 acres of green space AT SCHOOL is a complete*
> *game changer. They come here every day. Building*
> *programming and instruction around that space, we hope*
> *to see real changes in health and academic outcomes.*
>
> —Shane Allison

> *I don't know anything about nature. I wanted to be*
> *in the spring park program because I just wanted to*
> *belong to something. I felt like this park could make*
> *a difference in the community. But after working on*
> *the park for a month, I realize how much I personally*
> *needed the park. I feel connected to the world.*
>
> —Cara, sophomore enrolled in the initial Spring
> Community STEM Pilot Program

Source: Photo by Andrew McClellan. Used with permission.

Andrew McClellan teaches a fourth-, fifth-, and sixth-grade self-contained class at a North Avondale Montessori school. A communications major in college, he discovered his love for nature-based education when doing a marketing and PR internship for the local nature center. This inspired him to earn a master's degree in education and begin teaching in public school. Andrew integrates his passion for the outdoors into the Montessori philosophy, helping students not only learn about the environment but also consider their relationship with it. He incorporates the outdoors whenever possible. For example, he often takes their Friday community meetings outdoors, where he notes that conversations tend to be more open because the background sounds provided by nature seem to make students more likely to add their voices to the conversation. Through a supplemental position as the outdoor resource coordinator of the school, Andrew creates and maintains natural areas on school grounds for all classes to use.

I love seeing the change in my students when we extend our learning experiences into outdoor spaces. Whether it's for the purpose of a read-aloud, a science experiment, or simply a brain break, I've always found an outdoor setting opens up new possibilities.

—Andrew McClellan

STUDENT-CREATED OUTDOOR CLASSROOM

Source: Photo by Jenny Herkins. Used with permission.

When Jenny Herkins's second graders came up with the idea to take learning outdoors in response to the COVID pandemic, she let them take the lead. She asked them to think about what an outdoor class-room would need, and they explored the schoolyard to find a space. They found a wooded area that students thought was perfect, and she guided them through the process of determining the "time, talent, and treasure" that would be necessary to complete such a big project. Students and parents donated their time on the evenings and weekends; a talented Eagle Scout built picnic tables, benches, and a covered whiteboard; and treasure came in the form of mulch, wagons, tools, and fencing donated by a local hardware store. The outdoor classroom has a large meeting area with benches and small "breakout rooms" with spools donated by the electric company that serve as tables. Over three school years, three of Jenny's second-grade classes and their families have added to this project to create what is now a beautiful, functional outdoor classroom that can be used by all the classes in the school.

> *My classes have learned so much through this project. We have written countless letters, done research on various topics, worked together to make an impact to get our needs met, changed the environment in a positive way, and so much more. Not only have my students learned content in our social studies, science, and language arts curriculum, they now know that their efforts make a difference!*

> —Jenny Herkins

FROM HORTICULTURALIST TO INTERVENTION SPECIALIST

Source: Photo by Bryna Bass. Used with permission.

When Bryna Bass graduated college with a degree in agriculture, she never realized that she would eventually transition from growing plants to growing students. Bryna is an intervention specialist in an elementary school multiple disability and autism unit. She shares her passion for plants with her students by involving them in the thriving school gardens, which she helped create over 10 years ago. She notes that taking her students outdoors is a calming experience for them and that nonverbal students especially seem to like the sensory piece of being outdoors because it engages all of their senses. The garden also provides hands-on learning opportunities that don't require fine motor skills. Bryna likes how being outdoors can give students choices based on what they need or how they are feeling. She says that even 10 minutes outside can provide a soothing experience and help her students renew and reset before they begin a new lesson or task.

> *Outdoor experiences offer a good balance of freedom and structure. Adults model for children all of the time, and this is particularly true for children with disabilities. The garden is the perfect place to employ all of the senses while learning about the world.*
>
> —Bryna Bass

URBAN OUTDOOR CLASSROOM

Source: Photo by Ryan Britton. Used with permission.

Elementary school principal Ryan Britton has witnessed the benefits of outdoor time with students throughout his teaching career. When this former kindergarten teacher became a principal, he was determined to bring nature to students at his new school, despite it being located on Main Street in an urban area. He worked with a group of 20 dedicated teachers who expressed interest in his nature initiative to create an outdoor classroom in front of the school. Funded by a federal grant and community donation match, they worked with a local landscaping company and the school custodial staff to come up with creative ways to build an outdoor space that was accessible to all. Covering the area with synthetic turf on top of several inches of sand made the outdoor classroom wheelchair accessible. Fiberglass "rock" seats were much more affordable than bringing in real rocks, and the area is surrounded by three seasons of flowering native plants. Teachers of all grades use the area for various learning experiences, and occupational therapists and physical therapists use the area to help students meet certain motor goals. Next, the school plans on adding bird feeders to their campus so that fifth and sixth graders can join Project FeederWatch (see Appendix), a citizen science project from the Cornell Lab. A few instances of theft of some non-permanent materials have occurred, but this has not deterred Ryan from providing these outdoor learning spaces for students. Instead, his reaction is to bring more members of the community into the outdoor learning spaces so that the whole neighborhood feels connected to them.

> As an urban school, we often overlook the nature surrounding our schools but are given an opportunity to teach beyond our four walls and connect with nature, which is always around us. From insects joining students while reading a book in the grass or on turf, to a bird flying overhead, to a soft breeze cooling you down on a warm day: an outdoor classroom opens up the possibilities our students see in the world around them.
>
> —Ryan Britton

OUTDOOR LEARNING IN THE SNOW

Susan Koch's first graders spend half of a day in the forest each week, hiking, playing, singing, and learning. Her school partnered with the North Branch Nature Center to create an outdoor learning program called ECO: Educating Children Outdoors. All pre-K through fourth-grade students participate in the program year-round, even in the cold, snowy New England winters. The school has a lending library of extra outdoor clothing in the basement that the parents wash and maintain, and the PE department even has two

Source: Photo by Marita Frey. Used with permission.

class sets of snowshoes. Susan emphasizes the importance of doing a safety assessment of your outdoor space before taking students and recommends reaching out to local tree experts, park staff, or nature centers to help with that. Children follow a routine for their ECO time each week, and Susan teaches them to remember the 3Cs, or 3 Cares: (1) I care for myself, (2) I care for others, and (3) I care for Earth. She did her graduate work on multilingual learners and outdoor education and now teaches an ECO Educator Institute each summer to share her expertise and experiences with other educators.

Nature is a powerful teaching partner. Creativity, collaboration, communication, and critical thinking are all required and fostered in outdoor classrooms. I encourage educators to explore the possibilities of outdoor learning, whether it be in the schoolyard, park, forest, or meadow. The possibilities are endless for fostering Earth stewards and future leaders.

—Susan Koch

BRINGING THE OUTDOORS IN

When you walk from the bustling city streets into Arlitt Child Development Center, your setting is quickly transformed into a peaceful, fresh learning environment. Beautiful green foliage is present throughout the school, and preschool teacher Beulah Cable is known as the plant whisperer. Her classroom is filled with a variety of plants, many of which have been given to her by teachers, school families, and friends. Students help care for the plants and watch them grow and change. She says that the plants not only create an inviting atmosphere and rich learning opportunities for students but also absorb some of the sounds of a busy preschool classroom. Beulah recommends starting with plants that are easy to care for and making sure they are non-toxic before bringing them into the classroom.

> *I love having the plants in my room. They improve the air quality, literally helping me breathe more deeply, and they give me hope with their constant renewal of life.*
>
> —Beulah Cable

Source: Photos by Pamela Blanchard. Used with permission.

Dr. Pamela Blanchard, an associate professor of education at Louisiana State University, helped start a program called LSU Coastal Roots in which students play an integral part in protecting Louisiana's eroding coastline. At their schools, students help install a 10-ft × 10-ft native plant nursery for growing dune grass and native trees whose roots help hold soil in place. Students tend to the plants throughout the school year, and when the plants are ready, they travel to their restoration site to plant them. Through this innovative stewardship program, students are learning school curriculum in a meaningful way while developing a connection with their land. Teachers typically participate in the program year after year, and Pam says there is an oral history that occurs when teachers bring students to their restoration site to plant each year. When teachers show their students plantings other classes before them have made, students realize they are doing something that matters. Several students who have graduated high school come back to help with the trips. Pam shares that there are many place-based environmental stewardship programs for students to be involved in, such as stream quality monitoring, removing invasive plant species, and raising and releasing native fish, and recommends your state Department of Natural Resources as a great place to start. The LSU Coastal Roots program looks a little different at each school because Pam lets the teachers plan the program the way that works best for them and their students.

I love to be a witness to all the creative thinking that goes on when you just let teachers be teachers.

—Dr. Pam Blanchard

BRING ON THE BEES

Source: Photos by Kristy Giplin. Used with permission.

When media specialist Kristy Gilpin told her district superintendent, "I want to bring bees into the school," he wasn't sure what to think! Kristy wanted to help students understand the importance of pollinators, so she applied for a grant from Whole Foods for her school to be part of the Bee Cause Project (see Appendix). She worked with the administration, the custodial staff, and a local beekeeper mentor (who just happened to be the school secretary's husband) to set up a bee observation hive in one of the school's classrooms. During their library time, all 800 students were able to observe the bees, read about them, learn about their sophisticated social system, and hear about the process of pollination. Kristy noticed that the students who were afraid of bees became less fearful as they learned more about them. The year the bee hive was installed, the entire school celebrated with a week-long pollinator-palooza filled with activities about bees and other pollinators and culminating in a dress like your favorite pollinator day!

> *In lower grade levels, the bulk of what we do is about exposure, connections, and enthusiasm. Our beehive gave students an opportunity to explore, observe, and understand how living things impact their daily lives.*
>
> —Kristy Gilpin

WOODSY WEDNESDAYS

Source: Photos by Amy Poor. Used with permission.

Amy Poor's kindergarten students are ready for adventure when they come to school on Wednesdays. Amy has designated the day as Woodsy Wednesday, a day she and her students spend at least an hour learning in the woods on their school grounds. Amy has found that establishing a routine for this extended outdoor time helps students feel comfortable and excited when they go outside. They always begin sitting in a circle and singing a song. Then, they participate in a lesson that integrates nature and end with a game or free exploration time. When asked how she keeps track of all those kindergartners, Amy said she teaches her students to travel like a school of fish, for the same reasons that fish do—to keep everyone safe. To come up with ideas for Woodsy Wednesday lessons, Amy takes short walks outdoors with the grade-level standards in mind, and something outside usually sparks a lesson idea. Woodsy Wednesdays take place throughout the seasons and in all types of weather.

Getting outside on a regular basis helps me be a better teacher! I personally can tap into some of the same benefits my students get by getting outside, like fresh air, higher engagement, enhancing my curiosity and wonder, and growing love and respect for the natural world around me.

—Amy Poor

Cultivating Green Space at Your School

As you think about how you might add more green space to your schoolyard, keep in mind the partners you might work with to bring your ideas to reality. Would your PTO/PTA be interested in sponsoring a green space? Which community organizations might want to be involved in planning and creating this space? Would a local university, nature center, parks department, or landscaping business want to form a partnership? Do you know of any Scouts who are looking for Eagle Scout or Gold Award projects? Partnerships can help financially and ease the workload involved in making your green project happen, and they can also foster connections within the community. Invite teachers, administrators, office staff, anyone from the school who is interested, to take part in the project. Remember to include your custodial staff in the planning process, as they will likely have some creative ideas about what will work best on your school grounds.

Invite your students and their families to get involved. Many of the educators I talked to said they were pleasantly surprised by the

Source: Photo by Jenny Herkins. Used with permission.

willingness of families to share their tools, talents, and weekend time to help create green spaces. Not only are they creating spaces for their children to learn, they are also making memories with their kids as they do this work together.

Connecting With Nature in a Traditional School Setting

When high school history teacher Meredith Florkey was looking for the best early childhood learning opportunities for her two young children, she discovered the benefits of outdoor learning. This secondary teacher turned her focus to early childhood, earning a master's degree in nature-based early childhood education. She founded Ohio Naturally, an organization that focuses on teacher training, community building, advocacy, and consultation in order to increase the capacity of nature-based early childhood education in her state. Meredith has combined her experience working in a traditional school setting and her expertise in nature-based education to help schools incorporate outdoor learning into conventional school days. Meredith has some great advice for anyone wanting to integrate nature time at school:

The most important thing to keep in mind when approaching standard public education settings to incorporate nature is to lean in with curiosity and be flexible.

Keep your goal in mind: to increase quality time outdoors; then identify classroom, building, and district goals and align the two.

Next identify your stakeholders (your two most important allies are the school secretary and custodian) and those who already love and see the value in nature to also work on your curious and flexible team.

Realize that these efforts will not move forward with a "someone should really do that" mentality; you will need to do the in-between, often non-glamorous work.

And lastly, lead past your time, as you go along, make sure that there are folks who will be at the building after you are involved, that you document everything, and engage local leaders in your parks department, service groups, and local government.

—Meredith Florkey

Incorporating Nature in Urban Schools

Connecting students with nature in urban settings can be more challenging than in rural or suburban settings due to the lack of green space. However, I have encountered many educators who have come up with creative ways to bring nature to students in urban settings, and one recurring piece of advice is to start small but with a vision. For example, after the staff of Arlitt Child Development Center did an all-staff book study on Richard Louv's *Last Child in the Woods* led by center director Dr. Victoria Carr, they were committed to bringing nature experiences into their urban preschool. Their initiative started simply with some pots and a worm bin. Each classroom received a pot and committed to planting something in it that first year, and teacher Rachel Konerman was brave enough to start a worm bin in her classroom for students to observe. A little more nature was added each year: indoor plants, tree stump seats on the playground, a fish tank, and eventually a nature playscape. Fifteen years later, nature is infused in everything they do at Arlitt. Each classroom is named after a native tree, rocks with students' names are used to take attendance, plants grace every classroom, sand and shells fill sensory tables, racks of rain jackets and buckets of boots are available for all-weather outdoor play, shelves are filled with natural objects found by teachers or brought in by families, and the list goes on. Konerman, now the professional development coordinator at the school, emphasizes the role of documentation in keeping families in the loop about their nature-based initiatives. She said teachers take photographs of students engaging with nature—be it observing earthworms, holding pill bugs, or making mud pies—and display them along with students' writings and drawings about the activities so families can see how meaningful these activities are to their children.

Source: Photos by Rachel Konerman. Used with permission.

For some of the children we work with, nature is very difficult to access. Some of them have never been barefoot in the grass until they play in our nature playscape. The joy they feel when exploring nature builds a foundation for learning about all sorts of things, including science and math, themselves and each other, and it stays with them long after they leave our center.

—Rachel Konerman

If you teach in an urban school district, incorporating nature might seem like a daunting task, but it is okay to start small. Simple things like bringing some plants in or caring for an outdoor pot of pollinator-friendly flowers might be a great place to begin.

Resources to Get Started

bit.ly/3HfQGn8

The Children & Nature Network has a Green Schoolyard Hub that includes practical resources for creating green spaces in a variety of school settings. The hub features a Green Schoolyards Toolkit comprised of case studies, advocacy materials, funding options, and planning guides.

Scan the first QR code on this page to access the Children & Nature Network Green Schoolyard Hub.

https://www
.greenschoolyards
.org/

Green Schoolyards America is another organization that provides helpful resources such as free schoolyard activity guides, an outdoor learning library, and opportunities to get involved in advocacy for green schoolyards. Scan the second QR code on this page to access Green Schoolyards America.

There are so many ways to get students outdoors and foster connections with nature. Whether you do small things like bringing in a few plants or big projects like creating an outdoor classroom, every effort matters.

GREEN TIME FOR YOU

5

*Almost everything will work again if you unplug
it for a few minutes, including you.*

—Anne Lamott

It is important to remember that the benefits of green time apply to
you, too. Just 5 minutes outdoors can refresh, renew, and reset your
mind and body. This chapter includes ideas on how to fit in some
green time for yourself both at school and at home.

Green Time at School

Source: iStock.com/Goodboy Picture Company

TAKE THE GREEN BREAKS WITH YOUR STUDENTS

If possible, do the green breaks activities along with your students.
It is good for your mental health and good modeling for them. You
might even share your observations, drawings, or nature journal
entries with them. This can make the time even more special and
strengthen your connection with each other.

TAKE YOUR OWN GREEN BREAKS

Teacher breaks are few and far between, but we can make the most of them by making some of them green breaks. As you are brainstorming green breaks for yourself, reflect on the four components of attention restoration theory (Kaplan & Kaplan, 1989) shared in Chapter 2: being away, soft fascination, extent, and compatibility.

Then ask yourself the following questions:

- What nearby green space can I visit to *be away* from the setting that is draining my attention?

- What is something I can do in that green space to experience *soft fascination* (activities that hold my attention effortlessly)?

- What can I do to experience the *extent* of being fully immersed in this setting?

- Does this setting feel *compatible* for me, in other words, am I completely comfortable in this space?

The answers to these questions will be different for all of us, so the green breaks we choose will be different. Finding a place that you can go to during the school day for your own personal green break can help you reset your mind, refresh your focus, and renew your patience.

GREEN DINING

Source: iStock.com/DisobeyArt

Consider eating your lunch outdoors. If you don't have a space outside to eat, work with your administrator, colleagues, and custodial staff to create a space where you all can enjoy lunch outdoors. Your PTO/PTA might even want to help. This dining space can be as simple as a picnic table or as elaborate as a covered shelter, and should be far from the playground and parking lot, so that you can feel "away" during your lunch.

CLASSROOM PLANTS

Bringing plants into the classroom can provide a more peaceful setting for you and your students. Choose plants that are easy to care for and that will survive over breaks during the school year, such as a ZZ plant, snake plant, pothos, or succulents. If you have very young students who might nibble on plants, be sure to choose plants that are nontoxic. For more info and some resources on classroom plants, see the green break titled "Bringing the Outdoors In" (see Chapter 3, p. 80).

Green Time at Home

We all know that your work does not end when you leave the school building, so I have included some green time ideas for home. When working in my home office, I can usually tell that it's time for a break when I grab my phone and start scrolling. And then I have to remind myself that scrolling is not going to renew my focus and refresh my mind like a green break would. During the COVID lockdown, my family created a native plant area in our backyard with a path that winds through it. A walk around this short path provides a nice green break where I can get away from my computer (the activity that is typically draining my attention), turn my attention to the natural setting, be fully immersed with all of my senses, and feel at ease. Even though I have walked this path over and over, I can usually notice something new each time I go.

CREATE YOUR OWN GREEN SPACE

Source: iStock.com/FluxFactory

Identify or create a green space where you can "get away" from the responsibilities of home. This can be a chair that sits under a tree in your yard, window box or pot of plants that you can tend to, a vegetable garden, or a path you can walk regularly. The key is that it is easily accessible for a short break. In other words, you don't have to get in the car or take a bus to get there. Practice some of the green break activities in this space. Look for something new every time you go—blooms, growth, wildlife. Engage your senses, drink your coffee, sit down for a few minutes, whatever you need that day.

CONSIDER SOME HOUSE PLANTS

Source: iStock.com/RgStudio

I recently discovered the joy of houseplants, but I must admit that I only buy the easy ones. Plants can add feelings of peace and freshness to your home and the weekly routine of watering and spritzing them serves as a nice green break. If you have pets, it is important to make sure the plants you bring in to your home are nontoxic to animals. The ASPCA has a website where you can access lists of nontoxic plants, or look up a particular plant to see if it is safe for pets. Scan the QR code on this page to access the site.

bit.ly/3LcllBV

EXPLORE YOUR LOCAL PARKS

Source: iStock.com/gbh007

For longer experiences in nature, or if you don't have access to green space in your neighborhood, explore your local parks. I am lucky to have a wetland park just a mile from my home. I have walked the loops around the ponds hundreds of times and never tire of the view. I find peace in the familiar sights, like the great blue heron that fishes there regularly, and excitement in seeing something new, like when the monarch caterpillars emerge to munch on the milkweed. Find out what parks are close by and choose some favorites that you can visit regularly, alone or with family or friends.

CONNECT WITH OTHERS

Source: iStock.com/DisobeyArt

If you want to enhance your experiences in nature, find some like-minded people to share these adventures. Your area might have local hiking clubs, birdwatching groups, or gardening groups.

You may want to connect with outdoor affinity groups and/or follow them on social media, such as the following:

- Color in the Outdoors: https://www.colorintheoutdoors.com/
- Disabled Hikers: https://www.disabledhikers.com/
- Diversify Outdoors: https://www.diversifyoutdoors.com/
- Latino Outdoors: https://latinooutdoors.org/
- Melanin Base Camp: https://www.melaninbasecamp.com/
- Outdoor Afro: https://outdoorafro.org/
- Native Women's Wilderness: https://www.nativewomenswilderness.org/
- Women's Wilderness: https://womenswilderness.org/

If you are interested in adding more green time to your family life, a great resource is Richard Louv's book, *Vitamin N: The Essential Guide to a Nature-Rich Life* (2016), which provides activities, resources, and inspiration for connecting with nature and your loved ones. And if you have small children, a family nature club might be a great way to connect with other nature-loving families. The Children & Nature Network offers a step-by-step guide to starting a family nature club. Scan the QR code on this page to access the guide.

bit.ly/3LbCPPM

DON'T UNDERESTIMATE THE POWER OF A HAMMOCK

My favorite green time place that I return to again and again is the hammock attached to two trees in my backyard, my happy place. Something about "floating" in this hammock in this little wooded area gives me the feeling of being totally immersed in nature and away from the busy-ness of life, even though it is just steps from my back door. Sometimes I take a book, sometimes I take a cold drink, and sometimes I take a nap. I realize that not everyone feels comfortable in a hammock, but you might want to give it a try. Just make sure it is well-made, securely attached to trees or posts, not too far off the ground, and has a soft area underneath.

I hope you will try some of these ideas to add more green time to your life. If this is something new for you, start small and see how the green breaks make you feel. Try some of these ideas with family or friends. Model for your own children how a green break can help them reduce stress and refocus. Most importantly, take care of yourself. You deserve some green time.

References

Kaplan, R., & Kaplan, S. (1989). *The experience of nature: A psychological perspective.* Cambridge University Press.

Louv, R. (2016). *Vitamin N: The essential guide to a nature-rich life.* Algonquin Books.

GREEN RESOURCES

Organizations

- **Children & Nature Network** A network of "leaders, educators, activists, practitioners and parents working to turn the trend of an indoor childhood back out to the benefits of nature—and to increase safe and equitable access to the natural world for all." https://www.childrenandnature.org/

- **The Greater Good in Education Program** Produced by UC Berkeley's Greater Good Science Center, this program offers free resources centered on "science-based practices for kinder, happier schools," many of them nature-based. High-quality lessons and activities for all grade levels and subjects are provided. https://ggie.berkeley.edu/

- **Green Schoolyards America** An organization whose mission is to "inspire and support systems change to transform asphalt-covered school grounds into living schoolyards that improve children's well-being, learning, and play, while strengthening

their communities' ecological health and climate resilience."
https://www.greenschoolyards.org/

- **Latino Outdoors** This organization's mission is to "inspire, connect, and engage Latino communities in the outdoors and embrace *cultura y familia* as part of the outdoor narrative, ensuring our history, heritage, and leadership are valued and represented." https://latinooutdoors.org/

- **National Environmental Education Foundation (NEEF) Greening STEM Hub** Provides tools and resources for engaging students in STEM lessons that focus on real-world challenges with the natural environment. bit.ly/3Na2r2i

- **North American Association for Environmental Education** A membership-based organization that promotes environmental education throughout North America and is "dedicated to strengthening the field of environmental education and increasing the visibility and efficacy of the profession." https://naaee.org/

- **Outdoor Afro** This organization "celebrates and inspires Black connections and leadership in nature." https://outdoorafro.org/

- **Outside for 5** Take the pledge to spend at least 5 minutes a day, 5 days a week, outside with your students. https://www.outsidefor5.com/

Apps

- **Seek by iNaturalist** "Uses the power of image recognition technology to identify the plants and animals all around you." bit.ly/3n2TCwy

- **Merlin Bird ID from the Cornell Lab** "Answer three simple questions about a bird you are trying to identify and Merlin will give you a list of possible matches." https://merlin.allaboutbirds.org/

Nature-Based Citizen Science Projects

- **CitizenScience.gov** Provides a database of federally funded citizen science projects. https://www.citizenscience.gov/

- **Nature's Notebook** Students can observe and report seasonal changes in plants and animals. https://www.usanpn.org/natures_notebook

- **Project FeederWatch** Bird count program through the Cornell Lab of Ornithology. https://feederwatch.org/

- **Tree Campus K–12 from the Arbor Day Foundation** Start a Tree Campus Team in your school, and apply to have your school recognized as an Arbor Day Foundation Tree Campus. bit.ly/3Ng4wtv

Recommended Books for Educators

- *1000 Hours Outside: Activities to Match Screen Time With Green Time* (2022), by Ginny Yurich

- *Asphalt to Ecosystems: Design Ideas for Schoolyard Transformation* (2010), by Sharon Gamson Danks

- *Last Child in the Woods: Saving Our Children From Nature Deficit Disorder* (2008), by Richard Louv

- *Naturally Inclusive: Engaging Children of All Abilities Outdoors* (2022), by Ruth Wilson

- *The Nature Principle: Reconnecting With Life in a Digital Age* (2012), by Richard Louv

- *Nature Swagger: Stories and Visions of Black Joy in the Outdoors* (2022), by Rue Mapp

- *The Sense of Wonder: A Celebration of Nature for Parents and Children* (2017), by Rachel Carson, photographs by Nick Kelsh

- *Wildlife Ranger Action Guide: Track, Spot & Provide Habitat for Creatures Close to Home* (2020), by Mary Kay Carson

Recommended Children's Books

- *Anywhere Farm* (2017), by Phyllis Root, illustrated by G. Brian Karas

- *Finding Wild* (2016), by Megan Wagner Lloyd, illustrated by Abigail Halpin

- *Growing Patterns: Fibonacci Numbers in Nature* (2010), by Sarah C. Campbell

- *Harlem Grown: How One Big Idea Transformed a Neighborhood* (2020), by Tony Hillery, illustrated by Jessie Hartland

- *If You Find a Rock* (2008), by Peggy Christian, illustrated by Barbara Hirsh Lember

- *Jayden's Impossible Garden* (2021), by Mélina Mangal, illustrated by Ken Daley

- *Mysterious Patterns: Finding Fractals in Nature* (2014), by Sarah C. Campbell

- *Nature Did It First: Engineering Through Biomimicry* (2020), by Karen Ansberry, illustrated by Jennifer DiRubbio

- *Next Time You See* series by Emily Morgan, including *Next Time You See a Seashell* (2013), *Next Time You See a Sunset* (2013) available in Spanish, *Next Time You See a Firefly* (2013), *Next Time You See a Pill Bug* (2013) available in Spanish, *Next Time You See the Moon* (2014) available in Spanish, *Next Time You See a Maple Seed* (2014), *Next Time You See a Spiderweb* (2015), *Next Time You See a Cloud* (2016), *Next Time You See a Bee* (2019)

- *Our Tree Named Steve* (2007), by Alan Zweibel, illustrated by David Catrow

- *Outside In* (2020), by Deborah Underwood, illustrated by Cindy Derby

- *Step Gently Out* (2012), by Helen Frost and Rick Lieder

- *A Way With Wild Things* (2020), by Larissa Theule, illustrated by Sarah Palacios

- Weather Walks Series, by April Pulley Sayre, includes *Raindrops Roll* (2015), *Feel the Fog* (2020), *Best in Snow* (2016), and *Full of Fall* (2017)

- *What Is Symmetry in Nature?* (2011), by Bobbie Kalman

- *Wonderful Nature, Wonderful You* (2017), by Karin Ireland, illustrated by Christopher Canyon

Recommended Nature Poetry Books

- *All the Wild Wonders: Poems of Our Earth* (2010), edited by Wendy Cooling, illustrated by Piet Grobler
- *Black Nature: Four Centuries of African American Nature Poetry* (2009), edited by Camille T. Dungy
- *Devotions: The Selected Poems* (2020), by Mary Oliver
- *The Illustrated Emily Dickinson Nature Sketchbook* (2016), illustrated by Tara Lilly
- *National Geographic Book of Nature Poetry: More than 200 Poems With Photographs That Float, Zoom, and Bloom!* (2015), edited by J. Patrick Lewis, former U.S. Children's Poet Laureate
- *Outside Your Window: A First Book of Nature (2012)*, by Nicola Davies, illustrated by Mark Hearld

Green Curriculum Programs

- **The BEETLES Project** Resources designed for outdoor program leaders and field instructors from the Lawrence Hall of Science. http://beetlesproject.org/
- **Growing Up WILD** Provides nature-based lessons for children ages 3 to 6. bit.ly/3HgmxEk
- **Project WILD** Offers wildlife-based environmental education curriculum that fosters responsible actions toward wildlife and related natural resources. https://www.fishwildlife.org/projectwild
- **Project WET** Offers a comprehensive collection of water education books, guides, maps, posters, and downloadable resources. https://www.projectwet.org/

Green Grants

- **Seed Your Future** A comprehensive list of grants to support horticulture and garden programs in schools and youth programs. bit.ly/40Iz1LA

- **The Bee Cause Project** Offers honey bee grants, pollinator literacy grants, and pollinator habitat grants. https://www.thebeecause.org/

Professional Development

- **eePRO Online Platform for Environmental Education Professional Development** https://eepro.naaee.org/
- **NOAA Professional Development Opportunities for Teachers** bit.ly/3oNqQjQ
- **OutTeach Professional Learning Program** https://www.out-teach.org/
- **Outdoor Learning in Cold Weather Webinar from Antioch University** bit.ly/3L9OsqH
- **Project Atmosphere from the American Meteorological Society** https://www.ametsoc.org/index.cfm/ams/ education-careers/education-program/k-12-teachers/ project-atmosphere
- **Project Learning Tree** https://www.plt.org/trainings
- **Project WET Online Trainings** bit.ly/3Nj6KZ5
- **Project WILD Workshop Coordinators by State** bit.ly/40CLSit

Available for download at
**resources.corwin.com/
BalanceScreenTimeWithGreenTime**

Bring
Emily Morgan
to Your School
or District

School or Library Visits

A visit from an author can be a special experience for children, teachers, and parents. Emily's school and library visits focus on the science behind the books, the research that goes into nonfiction writing, and the process of writing a picture book. Emily also does hands-on science activities with children that will enhance their experience with the books.

Teacher Workshops

In her "Next Time You See" teacher workshops, Emily models science and reading activities that can be done before and after reading the books in her series. All of the activities are aligned to the Common Core State Standards for English Language Arts as well as *A Framework for K–12 Science Education*. As the co-author of the Picture-Perfect Science series, Emily has spent the past 10 years facilitating engaging, practical, and enjoyable teacher workshops nationwide.

Conferences

Emily's "Next Time You See" conference sessions feature one or two of her books and include activities to do with students before and after reading. Her keynote address, titled "Never Stop Wondering," encourages teachers and students to keep their minds open to new learnings and to be willing to change their preconceptions when they encounter new evidence. In this talk, she also explores the beauty of never-ending questioning in science—particularly the notion that the more you learn, the more questions you have.

For more information, visit emilymorganbooks.com

A SAGE Publishing Company

Helping educators make the greatest impact

CORWIN HAS ONE MISSION: to enhance education through intentional professional learning.

We build long-term relationships with our authors, educators, clients, and associations who partner with us to develop and continuously improve the best evidence-based practices that establish and support lifelong learning.